Gods, Goddesses, and Mythology

Volume 7

Mesopotamia–Nyx

Marshall Cavendish
New York • London • Singapore

Marshall Cavendish
99 White Plains Road
Tarrytown, New York 10591

www.marshallcavendish.us

© 2005 Marshall Cavendish Corporation

Library of Congress Cataloging-in-Publication Data

Gods, goddesses, and mythology/editor, C. Scott Littleton.
    p. cm.
    Includes bibliographical references and index.
    ISBN 0-7614-7559-1 (set : alk. paper)
1. Mythology--Encyclopedias. I. Littleton, C. Scott. II. Marshall
Cavendish Corporation. III. Title.

    BL312.G64 2005
    201'.3'03--dc22

2004040758

ISBN 0-7614-7559-1 (set)
ISBN 0-7614-7566-4 (vol. 7)

Printed and bound in China

09 08 07 06 05   6 5 4 3 2

General Editor
C. Scott Littleton, Occidental College, Los Angeles

Marshall Cavendish
Project Editor: Marian Armstrong
Editorial Director: Paul Bernabeo
Production Manager: Alan Tsai

Brown Reference Group
Project Editor: Chris King
Editors: Andrew Campbell, Henry Russell, Lee Stacy,
    Dawn Titmus
Designer: Steve Wilson
Picture Researcher: Helen Simm
Cartographer: Mark Walker
Indexer: Kay Ollerenshaw
Managing Editor: Tim Cooke

CONTENTS

MESOPOTAMIA

Mesopotamia (Greek for "land between the rivers") is the region between the Tigris and Euphrates rivers in what is now Iraq, northern Syria, and southern Turkey. Mesopotamia was one of the areas in which civilized human societies first developed about 5500 BCE. The fertile plains made up for the lack of rainfall and supported agriculture that formed the basis of a number of successive civilizations. Mud from the two great rivers was used to make bricks for building some of the world's earliest cities.

The early civilizations of Mesopotamia were built along the banks of two rivers, the Tigris and the Euphrates, which both rise in western Turkey and flow southward into a common delta on the Persian Gulf. Their spring flooding was always unpredictable and could not reliably be used for irrigation. A further difficulty caused by the floods was salinization. The salts in the sediment carried by the rivers spread out across the floodplain and marshland instead of draining into the sea. The water left by the floods evaporated, leaving the salts behind and eventually creating a saline desert that was useless for farming. This was especially true in areas that were irrigated. This problem was reflected in many aspects of Mesopotamian culture and religion. For example, the groundwater, especially that of the marshland in southern Mesopotamia, was sometimes personified as a god named Abzu (in Sumerian) or Apsu (in Akkadian).

Below: The Tigris River flows through southern Iraq on the way to its confluence with the Euphrates River.

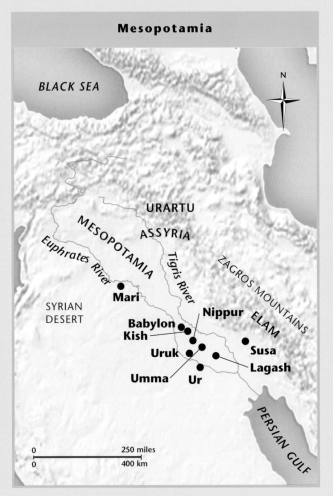

Mesopotamia

In Mesopotamia, the most prominent gods were those associated with water and fertility, and the most powerful were those that could overcome disorder, most notably the chaos caused by unpredictable spring floods. Since civilized life was possible only after the waters had been controlled, the gods that governed water were also regarded as being in charge of creative culture. Thus, for example, Enki (later known as Ea in Akkadian), whose name may mean "Lord Earth," was not only a god of fresh water but also a patron of arts, crafts, and intellectual activities.

Trading contacts

Mesopotamia is bounded to the east by the Zagros Mountains and to the west by the Syrian desert. To the north are the highlands of Anatolia (part of modern Turkey). These topographical features were all great natural barriers to trade, so the main method of transportation and travel was by river. On reaching the Persian Gulf, ships could sail east and south as far as India, then west to the areas along the Arabian peninsula and east Africa. From all these areas products such as spices, resins (for perfume), rare woods, gold, and other valuable items were traded. From a

very early period, the people of Mesopotamia brought back the precious gemstone lapis lazuli from places such as Afghanistan and obsidian from the mountains of Turkey. Of course, not only luxury items were traded but also essentials such as copper, tin (to make the alloy bronze), and later iron.

Sumerians

The earliest of the ancient cultures of Mesopotamia was that of Sumer. The Sumerians were based in the southern part of what is now Iraq and spoke their own language. They were not organized into a single state, so there was no country (in the modern sense) known as Sumer or Sumeria. What we now call Sumeria consisted of many independent city-states, each governed by its own ruler and having its own patron god or goddess. The first historical periods of Sumer for which we have records are known as Early Dynastic Period I (2900–2700 BCE), Early Dynastic Period II (2700–2600 BCE), and Early Dynastic Period III (2600–2350 BCE). During this time there were several dominant cities. These were Ur, Uruk, Nippur, Lagash, and Umma. Umma and Nippur are the farthest north; Ur and Uruk are in the south; and Lagash is in the eastern area. None of these early city-states dominated the others until about 2500 BCE. At that time, the city of Kish, north of Umma, seems to have controlled several of its neighbors. Its rulers were the first to call themselves *lu-gal* ("king"). (Earlier rulers had called themselves *ensi*, or "priest-kings"). This seems to have inspired a later ruler of Lagash, who began his reign as lu-gal of Sumer by conquering Uruk. One of the great legends of Mesopotamian culture begins around this time. The ancient *Epic of Gilgamesh* may be based, at least in part, on a real king of Uruk who is thought to have lived around 2700 BCE.

The Sumerian civilization was one of the earliest societies, if not the first, to organize itself around urban centers, establish a bureaucracy, and develop systems of writing to record literature and mythology as well as day-to-day business transactions. The cities evolved around public buildings, particularly temples to the gods. These were an obvious focal point for the devotion of the citizens because every city had not only its own patron deity, but sometimes even its own pantheon of gods.

Writing was a most important tool in the creation of these civilizations. The work of scribes permitted the ruling class to keep track of economic transactions, including tax liabilities. However, there was more to writing than merely keeping a record of the movement of goods and money. Writing almost immediately became very important in

Some Gods of Mesopotamia

An: Also known as Anu (in Babylonian); sky god; among his numerous consorts are Ki (the earth) and various manifestations of the mother goddess.

Assur: Chief deity of the Assyrians; he often appears as a winged sun disk containing a bearded god holding a bow (but no arrow).

Ea: An early Akkadian deity, a later form of Enki; water god, creator god, god of wisdom and magic.

Enki: Sumerian earth god, also god of wisdom, arts, crafts, fate, and magic; later identified with Ea.

Enlil: God of air, wind, and storms.

Ereshkigal: Sumerian goddess of the underworld; sister of Inanna; wife of Gugulanna; later she is consort of Nergal and loses much of her power to him.

Inanna/ Ishtar: Goddess of love and war; consort of Dumuzi, god of fertility.

Marduk: Chief god of Babylon; credited with the organization of the universe.

Nergal: God of the underworld.

Ninhursag: One of the many manifestations of the mother goddess.

Ninlil: Sumerian goddess whose name means "Lady Air"; also known as Ninmah (meaning "great lady" in Sumerian); consort of Enlil and mother of Ninurta and Nanna.

Ninmah: Means "great lady" in Sumerian; one of the many manifestations of the mother goddess; also a title given to Ninlil and Ninhursag.

Ninurta: Identified with Ningirsu and later with Nabu; a warrior god who is also a god of rain and fertility.

Shamash: Also known as Utu (in Sumerian); sun god and god of justice.

Sin/ Nanna: (In Sumerian mythology) moon god of Babylon; son of Enlil and Ninlil; travels across the sky in a *gufa*, a small, canoelike boat made of woven twigs and tar, accompanied by the planets.

religion as a means of recording prayers, hymns, and myths. Previously these would have been passed down through oral tradition, but now many of the most important religious compositions were copied down onto clay tablets and thus preserved for posterity.

Originally the script invented by the scribes of Sumer was based on pictures. Over time, however, it evolved into thousands of symbols based on pictures but simplified into various lines and wedges. While the Sumerian writing system went through some changes, the materials used never varied. Clay was formed into tablets small enough to fit into the palm of a hand, and a sharp stylus was used to incise the tiny lines and wedges. The clay was usually baked to make it last longer. This writing system, known as cuneiform, could have been used on other materials, but, since there are few workable rock sources in southern Mesopotamia, inscriptions in stone are rare and usually occur only on decorative items such as seals and statues.

Other early civilizations

The Sumerians were not the only group to settle and grow powerful in Mesopotamia. A group of settlers speaking a Semitic language founded a city named Akkad (also known as Agade), which was located somewhere near modern Baghdad. Around 2300 BCE, Sargon, ruler of Akkad, created what might have been the first empire in western Asia. After subjugating the king of Lagash and becoming ruler of all the Sumerian states, Sargon marched north along the Euphrates River and "received kingship" from the god Dagon. Sargon and his successors introduced several changes to the concept of kingship. They were not merely kings of Akkad, but "kings of the four shores"—in other words, of the whole world. They received kingship from the gods, and they preceded their names with a cuneiform sign known as a determinative that had previously been used only with gods' names. These kings were also depicted wearing horned headdresses, just as gods would be. However, donning a divine tiara does not guarantee godlike powers. Sargon's son and successor faced a massive rebellion from his Sumerian subjects.

It was left to Sargon's grandson to reconsolidate the Akkadian Empire by replacing local rulers with his own administrators and reforming the writing and accounting procedures so that they would be standard throughout the empire. Both Sargon and his grandson Naram-Sin became figures in legend as well as history, and were written about for more than a thousand years. The mythology that grew up around Sargon's early years is particularly fascinating. According to the legends, Sargon's mother was a priestess;

his father's identity was unknown. His mother took the baby and placed him in a reed basket, which she set afloat on the Euphrates River. A wealthy man found the basket and adopted Sargon as his son, making him administrator over all his lands. Sargon received the kingship when the goddess Ishtar appeared to him and gave him her love. This story has parallels in many myths and traditions about historical and religious figures, including Moses in the Old Testament of the Judeo-Christian Bible and the twin founders of Rome, Romulus and Remus. The Akkadians integrated the myths and personalities of the Sumerian deities into their own religion, renaming them. For example, the Sumerian Inanna and Enki became the Akkadian Ishtar and Ea, respectively.

Dawn of a golden age

The rise of the Akkadians did not mean that the original Sumerian culture and language were dead. In fact, Akkadian control inspired something of a Sumerian renaissance. Gudea, king of the city-state of Lagash, began a golden age of art and monuments. He opened trade relations with countries beyond the Persian Gulf and imported materials to embellish the temples, especially those of his capital city, Girsu. The Third Dynasty of Ur became another great empire until it collapsed under the

Above: The ruins of Uruk. This ancient Sumerian city, first settled about 5000 BCE, lies 156 miles (250 km) southeast of Baghdad, Iraq.

weight of its own bureaucracy and was crushed by Amorite invasions. The Amorites were another non-Sumerian, Semitic-speaking group. They were originally nomads from Syria who settled in cities such as Isin, Larsa, Mari, Eshnunna, Halab (Aleppo), Qatna, and Babylon. From 2003 BCE to about 1595 BCE, they were so dominant that dynasties of Amorite kings reigned in all these cities. Because of this and because of the travels of traders, scholars, and government officials throughout the region, a single language, a dialect of Akkadian, became the common tongue of all the city-states under Amorite control. It was even written at such far-flung sites as Hazor (in modern Israel), Kanesh (in modern Turkey), and Susa (in modern Iran). Prior to the emergence of the Amorites, there had been thousands of languages in the region. From then on, languages related to Akkadian predominated.

The most important language became Babylonian. The First Dynasty of Babylon began its rule around 1900 BCE and remained in power until the Hittites, who came from the area of modern Turkey, invaded about 1600 BCE. The most famous king of Babylon was Hammurabi, whose name is associated with one of the most famous judicial

Left: This Sumerian statuette, thought to represent the sky god An, was carved about 2600 BCE.

codes of the ancient world. The laws of Hammurabi reveal much about the society for which they were written. They are also a valuable source of information about social norms for other periods of Mesopotamian history. Like all the cultures of this region in ancient times, the Babylonians had a strict social structure. Theirs consisted of three layers: *awilum* (citizens with property), *mushkenum* (a group required to give service to the state), and slaves. Like the laws of Moses in the Bible, the laws of Hammurabi were based on the principle of "an eye for an eye." Retaliation and harsh punishment for crimes remained the norm in subsequent Mesopotamian societies, and they were evidenced in many Mesopotamian myths.

The Babylonians were succeeded by rulers known today as Kassites, who retained the capital city at Babylon. Under the Kassites all of Mesopotamia was still dominated by the southern part of the territory. The Kassite kings reigned in the late 14th and early 13th centuries BCE, and were roughly contemporary with some of the most famous Egyptian pharaohs, including Akhenaton (ruled 1379–1362 BCE), Tutankhamen (ruled 1361–1352 BCE), and Ramses II (ruled 1304–1237 BCE). The origins of the Kassites are mysterious—they may have come from the Zagros Mountains to the east, on the border of modern Iran, or from somewhere on the Middle Euphrates. It is also possible that they were related linguistically to the Indo-European-speaking Aryans, who were invading northern India at about the same time. The Kassites brought with them their own language and gods, but they soon became assimilated by the Babylonians—politically they were in control, but culturally they were vanquished. In time they came to regard themselves as the guardians of their adopted society. In addition to restoring Babylonian temples, they encouraged the propagation of knowledge. Many scientific, literary, and religious works in Akkadian were collected and recopied during the 500 years of peaceful Kassite rule.

Aramaean invasions

In the 12th century BCE, the Aramaeans began a series of military incursions into Babylonian territory. The Aramaeans were a group of Semitic-speaking nomads who, like other Eurasian populations at this time, were migrating to new territories. This was the same time that the "Sea Peoples," a mixed group of warlike wanderers, began to push their way down the eastern coast of the Mediterranean Sea. No one knows for certain why so many peoples were on the move, but the effect on existing civilizations in their path was devastating. The historical city of Troy may have been destroyed at this time, and these invasions probably put an end to Mycenaean civilization as well. In Egypt, pharaoh Ramses III (ruled 1198–1166 BCE) was able to keep the hostile forces at bay, but not easily. Mesopotamia, while not invaded by the Sea Peoples, suffered damage at the hands of the Aramaeans. The Aramaeans reached the walls of the Assyrian city of Nineveh, and then seem to have sacked the city of Babylon itself. The most lasting impact of these invasions was the introduction of a new language. Aramaic would be spoken and written (on papyrus) throughout the area, although the kings of the neo-Assyrian and neo-Babylonian dynasties still insisted that official documents and letters be written in cuneiform text on clay tablets.

The ascent of Assyria

At the beginning of the first millennium BCE there was a power shift in Mesopotamia away from the south. A new group of warrior kings from the northern kingdom of Assyria began to dominate Mesopotamia and the surrounding areas. Assyria had originally been a small nation of farmers and herders, but in the Middle Assyrian Period (about the 14th century BCE), the civilization had managed to gain influence over a larger area. From about 1000 BCE to 612 BCE, through a combination of administrative and military skill—and ruthless brutality to those who opposed them—the Assyrians created an empire that filled the vacuum left by the gradual disintegration of other imperial powers such as Egypt, the Hittites, and Babylon.

The Babylonians and the Assyrians had very similar cultures and mythologies. However, the chief gods of their respective pantheons were different. Marduk was the head of the Babylonian pantheon, while Assur was chief of the Assyrian gods and gave the country its name. Marduk's origins were obscure. He is mentioned in very early Sumerian

documents, but the meaning of his name was a mystery even to the ancient Babylonian priests themselves. He does not seem to have become important until around the time of Hammurabi. That king's law code stated that Enlil and Anu appointed Marduk lord of "the multitude of people." Marduk was depicted as a friendly and approachable god, but it would not be until the period of the Kassite kings that he became popular outside of Babylon. As time went on he became more important and began to acquire many of the powers and symbols of Enlil and other gods. In the *Enuma Elish*, a creation myth written in its fullest form around 1150 BCE, Marduk was credited with the establishment of order in the universe. By the seventh century BCE, Marduk had become the official state god of the neo-Babylonian Empire. His temple and ziggurat were so magnificent that stories about them were recorded by

Right: The carving on this upright stone slab, or stele, depicts Hammurabi (left) receiving the laws from the sun god Shamash.

Seals

Ancient Mesopotamian ornamental seals were most often in the form of small cylinders of hard stone, with holes drilled through them lengthwise so that they could be threaded and worn like jewelry. Used to mark both official and private documents as authentic, they were sometimes kept and used for generations because of their beauty and value. In order to make an impression in a clay tablet or a wax or clay surface, the seal would be rolled over it like a tiny rolling pin, leaving both pictures and text as a raised design. In order to have the impression appear both raised and the right way around, the original image in the seal had to be carved deeply into the stone in a mirror image. Mesopotamian seals are often inscribed with the names of kings, and from this information it is often possible to establish the approximate date of their manufacture. Seals are also important sources for likenesses of the gods and goddesses, and scenes from the myths, of ancient Mesopotamia.

Greek historian Herodotus (c. 484–425 BCE) hundreds of years after Babylon was destroyed.

The process by which Marduk became the most important god in the pantheon and took up the powers and symbols of other, preexistent deities is typical of what happened in Mesopotamian culture in general as different groups rose to power. Depictions of Assur, patron god of the Assyrians, developed along similar lines. Originally Assur may have been a relatively insignificant mountain god, but as his worshipers gained power, they promoted him as well. When the Assyrians became a colonial power with an empire at their disposal, Assur acquired the characteristics and powers of several other gods, including Shamash, An, and Enlil.

In the tenth and ninth centuries BCE, the Assyrians began to reconquer their former territories from Babylon. These lands included Israel and other newly re-formed

Right: Carved about 645 BCE, this stone relief from the palace of Nineveh, an ancient city on the Tigris River, shows a royal banquet.

kingdoms along the Mediterranean coast. In addition, the Assyrians had to deal with other invaders, such as the Chaldeans (also known as the Kaldu) and the Elamites, and with the resurgent Babylonian state. The Elamites lived to the east and south of the Assyrians. Early in their history they had developed a writing system based on that of the Sumerians and Akkadians. Throughout the history of Mesopotamia, however, they were hostile to whichever group was in power.

Below: The stone seal (right) was used to make the impression (left) of Akkadian gods (about 2300 BCE).

Power changing hands

In Babylon itself, the Assyrians' greatest struggle was with the Aramaic-speaking Chaldeans, who had moved into the southern part of Mesopotamia, in the areas where the cities of Sumer had once flourished. As an ancient capital and a center of religion, Babylon was still very powerful. In the ninth century BCE the Assyrian king Shalmaneser III (ruled 858–824 BCE) reestablished the city's temples and encouraged a cultural renaissance there. In the following century, however, the Chaldeans succeeded in capturing Babylon, much to the Assyrians' dismay, but Chaldean dominance was not to last long: the great Assyrian king Tiglath-pileser III (ruled 745–727 BCE) drove the Chaldean ruler out of Babylon and set himself up as the sovereign of Babylonia, symbolically "taking the hand of Marduk" in the process. Tiglath-pileser III achieved great military victories over the neighboring nation of Urartu and the kingdoms of Syria. He and his successors would rule an empire that stretched from Susa in Persia (modern Iran) to Thebes in Egypt.

It is possible to argue that these political upheavals were reflected in the great epic poem *The Myth of Erra*, which was composed during this period. Erra was a weather god turned war god who raged against older deities such as Ea

and Marduk for having retired and given up their responsibilities. Erra then tried to take over the running of the world, but ended up devastating the cities of Mesopotamia until he decided to turn his powers against its enemies instead.

The Assyrians' new policy for conquered areas was to turn them into provinces, deport the original inhabitants, and replace them with deportees from other conquered regions (see box, page 877). This policy would have long-lasting cultural consequences as these people brought their traditions and beliefs to new areas. Babylon itself was the only exception to this policy. In 694 BCE the Babylonians handed over the son of the Assyrian king Sennacherib (ruled 704–681 BCE) to the Elamites. In response, Sennacherib decided on merciless punishments for his enemies, the Elamites and the rebellious Babylonians. In 689 BCE he conquered Babylon and destroyed much of the city.

The neo-Assyrian Empire eventually fell in 609 BCE, after years of continuous warfare with the Medes (who came from the area of modern Iran), the Babylonians, and the Egyptians. The Assyrian rulers were ousted by Babylonians, and the neo-Babylonian Empire was established. Perhaps the most famous of the neo-

Babylonian kings is Nebuchadnezzar II (ruled 605–562 BCE), who captured Jerusalem in 597 BCE. During his 43-year reign Nebuchadnezzar began an extensive building campaign, especially in Babylon. It was at this time that the magnificent Ishtar Gate was built in the city. Nebuchadnezzar seems to have been one of the few kings of Babylon who did not boast about the number of people he had massacred. Most of his energy seems to have gone into restoring the temples of the gods and reviving old traditions. From the inscriptions written during Nebuchadnezzar's reign, the king seems more like an archaeologist or scholar than a tyrant—he appears to have been principally concerned with clearing the ruins of old sanctuaries so that he could discover their original plan and duplicate them.

Nebuchadnezzar also took an interest in historical religious institutions. For example, he appointed his daughter high priestess of the moon god Sin in the ancient city of Ur. This same moon god would also play an important role in the fall of the empire during the reign of Nabonidus (died c. 539 BCE). Nabonidus was named after

Nabu, who had taken over some of the cosmic roles of the rain god Ninurta. Nabonidus claimed to have had a dream in which the moon god and Marduk in the form of the planet Jupiter appeared to him in the sky and told him to rebuild the temple to the moon in the city of Harran. When Nabonidus protested that he could not do this because the city had been captured by the Medes, Marduk told the king that a king of the Persians named Cyrus would liberate the city for him.

The fall of Babylon

Indeed, as it turned out, it was the Persian king Cyrus the Great (c. 585–c. 529 BCE) who ended the neo-Babylonian Empire in just a few years when he marched largely unopposed into the heart of the country. The fall of Babylon in 539 BCE ended the independence of Mesopotamia. It also marked the beginning of the end for the language and religion of Mesopotamia. Although the Persians were themselves supportive of the old languages and gods, the indigenous people began to drift away from the worship of Marduk and join the followers of the moon god Sin. Sin and his city remained powerful for more than 1000 years, until the rise of Islam in the seventh century CE.

Below: These tiles decorated the processional way to the Ishtar Gate in the ancient Mesopotamian city of Babylon.

Above: The inscription on this cuneiform tablet of the seventh century BCE describes movements of the planet Venus.

Jews in Mesopotamia

After the rise of Sumer, many different peoples settled in Mesopotamia; some prospered and came to dominate the region, while others were subjugated. From about 1000 BCE the Assyrian Empire that had spread throughout Mesopotamia and beyond began to crumble and was finally defeated by the neo-Babylonians in 612 BCE. The Persian king Cyrus II, called the Great (ruled c. 585–c. 529 BCE), then invaded Mesopotamia in 539 BCE and brought an end to neo-Babylonian control.

The Assyrians controlled aliens such as the Jews by splitting them up into small groups and deporting them to various parts of the empire. Dispersing a people in this way reduced the danger that discontented individuals might unite against the rulers. This policy was continued by the neo-Babylonians, who made sure that the Jews remained thinly distributed around Mesopotamia and the surrounding area.

The Persians had a policy of tolerance toward the conquered peoples. Exiled Jews were permitted safe return to Jerusalem—their capital that had been overrun by the Babylonians. Cyrus also allowed them to rebuild their temple in the city. The religious and social life of the Jews was not disturbed under Persian rule, and Jews traded freely around the Persian Empire.

In the Mesopotamian tradition, the collective of gods is known as the Annunaki or the Igigi. The Igigi sometimes seem to be the same as the Annunaki, but in other texts the Igigi are working at the command of the Annunaki. There seem to have been about 50 Annunaki, although this number varied. It was a group that usually consisted of senior gods such as Enlil, Enki, and An and various other deities. They were said in some stories to be the offspring of An, ranking somewhere in the middle echelon of deities. Some myths describe how they had to work for the great gods, and how they suffered hardships such as eating grass to allay their constant hunger. The Annunaki have almost as many roles as there are mentions of them. In *The Myth of Erra*, they are against humankind, but in a myth entitled *Enki and the World Order*, they pay homage to Enki and decree the fates of mortals. They are also judges in the story of Inanna's descent to the underworld.

LYN GREEN

Bibliography

Black, Jeremy, and Anthony Green. *Gods, Demons, and Symbols of Ancient Mesopotamia: An Illustrated Dictionary*. Austin, TX: University of Texas Press, 1992.

Roaf, Michael. *The Cultural Atlas of Mesopotamia and the Ancient Near East*. New York: Checkmark Books, 1990.

SEE ALSO: An; Creation Myths; Egypt; Enki; Enlil; Gilgamesh, Epic of; Inanna; Ishtar; Marduk; Ninurta.

MIDAS

In Greek mythology Midas was a king of Phrygia, part of what is now Turkey. He famously wished that everything he touched would turn to gold. When his wish was granted, Midas realized he had made a terrible mistake.

Above: This illustration by Arthur Rackham (1867–1939) captures the moment when Midas sees that he has turned his daughter into gold.

Although the stories about Midas are mostly myth and folklore, he was a real person. Also known as Mita, he ruled Phrygia in modern Turkey in the eighth century BCE, and archaeologists have found what they believe to be his tomb (see box, page 880).

In real life, as in legend, Midas was famed for his wealth as well as for his beautiful rose gardens. His kingdom, Phrygia, also known as Lydia or Mygdonia, was very prosperous. Midas is said to have founded the ancient city of Ancyra, which is now Ankara, the capital of Turkey.

The golden touch

The most famous story about Midas is the tale of his golden touch. According to this legend, Dionysus, the Greek god of wine, was passing through Phrygia when his old adviser, Silenus, a satyr, lost his way and ended up in Midas's gardens. Midas held a feast for Silenus, then helped him to find Dionysus again. To reward Midas for his help, Dionysus offered to grant him a wish.

Midas was very greedy, so he asked for everything he touched to be turned to gold. As promised, Dionysus granted his wish. At first, Midas was delighted with his golden touch. Then he realized that any food or drink he touched turned to gold too, and he could no longer eat or drink. He began to worry, and in despair he hugged his daughter, but she, too, turned to gold.

Midas soon asked Dionysus to undo his wish. Dionysus agreed and told Midas to go and bathe in the Pactolus River. Midas did so, taking his daughter with him. She was brought back to life and Midas was restored to normal. According to legend, ever since Midas touched its waters, the river has contained flecks of gold. Gold does naturally occur in the Pactolus River, and the story of Midas bathing in the river probably came about as a way of explaining the gold deposits there.

How Midas was given donkey's ears

Another story tells of how Midas was called upon to judge a music competition between Apollo (who was, among other things, the god of music) and Marsyas, a satyr. Apollo played his lyre, a harplike instrument, while Marsyas played a flute belonging to the goddess Athena. The other judges chose Apollo as the winner, but Midas disagreed and said

Marsyas should win. In another version of the story it was Pan, the fertility god, who competed with Apollo, playing on his panpipes.

In both versions of the tale, Apollo was furious with Midas for choosing his opponent and punished him for his poor judgment by giving him the ears of an ass. Midas was terribly ashamed of his huge ears and kept them covered with a turban. One person found out about them, however—the servant who cut the king's hair.

The servant was forbidden to gossip about the ears, but, desperate to tell the king's secret, he whispered it into a hole in the ground, which he then filled with earth. Reeds grew on the spot where the secret had been whispered, and every time the wind blew, the reeds repeated what the servant had said: "Midas has ass's ears." Midas became a laughingstock.

Above: This painting by Peter Paul Rubens (1577–1640) depicts Midas judging the music competition between Apollo and Pan.

The death of Anchurus

Despite the unfortunate things that happened to him, the mythical Midas never seemed to learn his lesson or acquire better judgment. According to one story, a huge hole opened up in the ground at a city named Celaenae. An oracle told Midas that he could only close the abyss by throwing his most precious possession into it. Midas still valued money above all else, and he threw vast amounts of gold and silver into the hole, but to no avail. His son, Anchurus, however, realizing that human life was more precious than anything, rode into the gaping hole on his horse. As the boy really was Midas's most precious possession, the hole closed up, and Midas lost his son forever.

The Tomb of Midas

What might be the 2,700-year-old tomb of the real King Midas was discovered in the 1950s near the small village of Yassihoyuk in central Turkey. The tomb was located under a conical hill, which is today known as the Midas Mound. Inside, archaeologists found the body of the old king, who probably died when he was about 60, lying on a thick layer of cloth inside a wooden coffin. With him in the tomb were items of wooden furniture as well as bronze goblets, bowls, pots, and pans—but nothing at all made of gold.

One of the most interesting things about Midas's tomb, however, was that it contained evidence of a huge funeral feast that would have been held to mark the king's death. Midas was buried with the dirty plates, cups, and utensils still in the tomb with him. By studying the leftovers, archaeologists have concluded that the feast probably included a spicy lamb stew, hummus (a paste made from chickpeas), broad-bean paste, halva (a dessert made from sesame seeds, honey, and nuts), and an alcoholic drink made from honey, grapes, and barley. In 2000, scientists re-created the original funeral menu for a Midas feast, which was held at the University of Pennsylvania Museum.

Below: This royal burial mound in Gordion, Turkey (formerly Phrygia), is similar to the one thought to house the body of Midas.

Midas himself is also said to have committed suicide by drinking bull's blood. According to different versions of the story, this was either because his kingdom was being invaded or because of his shame about his ass's ears.

Handing down the story

Several ancient writers mention Midas. They include Greek historian Herodotus (c. 484–425 BCE), Greek geographer Strabo (c. 64 BCE–23 CE), and Greek travel writer Pausanias (143–176 CE). The latter is thought to have come from the same region as Midas and wrote about him in his *Description of Greece*. Midas also appears in the work of Roman poet Ovid (43 BCE–17 CE) and that of Gaius Julius Hyginus, a Latin poet of the late first century BCE.

The tale of Midas's golden touch has been retold many times as a children's story, and he is often mentioned in literature as an example of someone who loves wealth. Attributing the "Midas touch" to someone can also refer to that person's ability to create wealth.

Midas has been depicted many times in art, especially in paintings showing the ill-fated music competition that he judged.

ANNA CLAYBOURNE

Bibliography
Pausanias, and Peter Levi, trans. *Guide to Greece*. New York: Viking Press, 1984.
Pinsent, John. *Greek Mythology*. London: Hamlyn, 1982.

SEE ALSO: Apollo; Athena; Dionysus; Pan; Satyrs; Silenus.

MINERVA

Originally an Etruscan deity of the dawn, in Roman mythology Minerva became the goddess of wisdom, arts and crafts, and war. When Minerva was later invested with many of the characteristics of the Greek goddess Athena, she was said to have sprung fully armed from the head of Jupiter.

Minerva was originally described as the daughter of Pallas, a giant whom she killed when he tried to rape her. The Romans soon identified Minerva with the Greek goddess Athena Promachos ("battle leader" or "champion"), and through that association she acquired her responsibility for the conduct of war. Minerva thus became an armed goddess, like Athena. Both deities carried a goatskin aegis bearing an image of the monstrous Gorgon head, the sight of which paralyzed enemy warriors with fear.

The Roman Minerva was also concerned with women's lives, especially domestic work such as spinning and weaving. In this capacity she was like Athena Ergane ("the worker"). Both goddesses also came to be associated with wisdom.

Below: This photograph shows the ruins of the three adjacent Roman temples of (left to right) Juno, Jupiter, and Minerva in Sbeïtla, Tunisia.

Left: This statue of Minerva forms part of the collection of ancient art treasures in the Capitoline Museum, Rome, Italy.

The origins of the Roman Minerva are elusive. According to Roman epic poet and dramatist Quintus Ennius (239–169 BCE), Minerva was one of the 12 great gods, which implied that she was Roman in origin. However, she did not appear in the earliest Roman religious calendars, a fact that has been taken as a clear indication that she was a goddess of exotic origin. In *De Lingua Latina* (*The Latin Language*), scholar Marcus Terentius Varro (116–27 BCE) claimed that Minerva came from Sabine territory, to the northeast of Rome. It is more likely, however, that the goddess came from Falerii (modern Civita Castellana), a city in southern Etruria (part of modern Umbria, in Italy). When Falerii fell to the Romans in 241 BCE, its cult of Minerva was transferred to Rome, where the goddess became known as Minerva Capta ("the captured"). A temple, the Minervium, was dedicated to her on the Caelian Hill in the city.

A goddess of importance

Regardless of whether she came to Rome from Etruria or was adopted by both civilizations from an independent source, Minerva was certainly one of the most important goddesses in the Etruscan pantheon. In Etruria her name was originally written as Menerva. Later it became Menrva, which is the form that appears on ancient vase paintings, sculptured reliefs, statues, and engraved bronzes.

Although her legend was almost certainly influenced by that of Athena, the Etruscan Menrva also shows traits that are not Greek in origin. Servius, a Latin grammarian of the fourth century CE, noted that Minerva could hurl lightning bolts, and the Etruscan Menrva was sometimes depicted carrying such weapons in her hand. Athena had no such power.

As Menrva, the goddess was worshiped at the Portonaccio sanctuary, which dates from the sixth century BCE, in the Etruscan city of Veii, about 12 miles (20 km) northwest of Rome. She was also worshiped in Santa Marinella, the ancient Punicum, a harbor of the Etruscan city Caere, which dates from about 540 BCE.

Beneath the altars of both these sanctuaries were channels that ran into the soil below, suggesting that the worship of Menrva was oriented to the earth. There seems also to have been a healing and probably an oracular aspect to her cult, which is indicated by the discovery of one of the lots that were used to predict the future. Small models of bodily organs and limbs offered to the goddess indicate that she was also seen as a healing divinity. Images of babies in swaddling clothes further suggest that one of the goddess's concerns was the welfare of children.

In her role as a warrior goddess, Minerva was often associated with Mars, the Roman god of war. Among the important archaeological relics unearthed at Praeneste—a town founded before the eighth century BCE in the Apennine Mountains north of Rome—is an engraved bronze container. Strongly influenced by Etruscan art, it bears an image of Minerva, who has put aside her shield and helmet and is tending the infant Mars. The child is naked except for his helmet, and he carries a shield. He is kneeling on the rim of a *pithos*, a large ceramic storage jar, in which depictions of what seem to be flames or moving water can be seen. Directly above Mars and the *pithos* is an image of Cerberus, the three-headed dog that guarded the entrance to the underworld. These symbols indicate that the *pithos* holds the water of the Styx River, which bordered the underworld and burned with fire. Minerva is carefully touching the lips of the little Mars with a styluslike instrument, anointing him with ambrosia, the divine food that gave the gods immortality.

The Etruscan Menrva frequently appears elsewhere in contexts that suggest the role of a children's nurse. Unlike the Greek Athena, Menrva is almost invariably a motherly figure, and there is little or no evidence that the Etruscans regarded her as the deity of handicraft and the arts, both of which roles she fulfilled in Athens and Rome.

Roman evidence of Minerva

From the mid-sixth century BCE, Minerva played an increasingly important role in the emerging Roman civilization. In Rome she shared with Juno a monumental presence on the Capitoline Hill in the great temple of Jupiter Optimus Maximus, which is traditionally dated to 509 BCE. The significance of Minerva's presence with Juno and Jupiter has never been entirely clear, although it may have been because all three deities were involved in the fall of Troy, from which the Romans believed that their ancestors had escaped.

Elsewhere in Rome substantial remains dating from about 530 BCE have been found at the Forum Boarium, a cattle market near the Tiber River. One of the artifacts unearthed there is a terra-cotta sculpture group depicting the helmeted Minerva standing beside the hero Heracles. It was originally

positioned on the roof of a temple that was almost certainly dedicated by King Servius Tullius (578–534 BCE) to the goddess Fortuna (the Roman goddess of fate, chance, and luck). The work probably represents the deification of Heracles. In this version he was introduced to the society of gods on Mount Olympus by Minerva. The inspiration for this scene came from Greek myths, which were probably brought to Rome by merchants from the east who frequented the markets near the port.

Other early images of Minerva have been found in ancient Lavinium (modern Pratica di Mare). Excavations there have brought to light a sanctuary of Minerva that dates to the second half of the sixth century BCE. Remarkable terra-cotta statues and two nearly life-size cult statues of Minerva from about 400 BCE confirm the

Right: This terra-cotta statue of the fourth century BCE comes from Lavinium and represents a female worshiper of Minerva.

Right: The goddess Minerva was depicted on Roman coins during the reign of Emperor Claudius I (41–54 CE).

importance of the goddess during this period. They show Minerva with a helmet, a round shield, and an aegis with the Gorgon head. Beside her body, which is entwined by a three-headed snake, is the small sea god Triton. This association with Triton occurs again in the epic poem the *Aeneid*, in which Roman poet Virgil (70–19 BCE) calls Minerva *Tritonia virgo* (Tritonian maid).

The sanctuary of Lavinium was for centuries a place of pilgrimage for Romans and other peoples of Latium. For them, Minerva was a goddess concerned with young men and, especially, young women at the time of their passage from adolescence to adulthood. The sumptuous gifts offered by her youthful worshipers at Lavinium underscore this aspect of her cult.

The Quinquatrus

The extent of Minerva's appeal to ordinary Romans is well illustrated by the expansion of her major festival. Originally a one-day annual event held on March 19, the Quinquatrus was gradually extended to five days of revelry. The date was originally also sacred to Mars, and although the rituals of Mars continued to be observed at the Quinquatrus, Minerva became the primary focus of the event.

March 19 was the dedication day of her temple (which archaeologists have never found) on the Aventine Hill in Rome, and a notation on an ancient calendar notes that it was the *artificum dies* ("day of the artisans"). According to Roman poet Ovid (43 BCE–17 CE), March 19 was Minerva's birthday, and on this date every year she was worshiped by all sorts of artists and craftspeople, but especially by boys and girls and their teachers, who enjoyed a five-day recess from school.

Minerva was a favorite of Emperor Domitian (ruled 81–96 CE). In his Forum Transitorium at Rome (also known as the Forum of Nerva), the goddess is pictured on a relief panel of the colonnade, surrounded by scenes of spinning and weaving. Minerva herself is shown in long, flowing robes, suggestive of the garments worn by musicians and performers—she was also the patroness of actors.

Whenever she first arrived in Rome, and wherever she came from, there can be little doubt that Minerva found her way into the hearts of all classes of Roman people.

DANIEL P. HARMON

Bibliography

Scheid, John, and Janet Lloyd, trans. *An Introduction to Roman Religion.* Bloomington IN: Indiana University Press, 2003.

Turcan, Robert, and Antonia Nevill, trans. *The Gods of Ancient Rome: Religion in Everyday Life from Archaic to Imperial Times.* New York: Routledge, 2001.

SEE ALSO: Aeneas; Athena; Gorgons; Juno; Jupiter; Mars; Rome; Triton.

MINOS

In Greek mythology Minos was the semidivine ruler of an empire based on the island of Crete. Although he is most famous for forcing the Athenians to send a small group of youths to Crete, where they were fed to a monster known as the Minotaur, Minos was viewed by some as a wise and just king.

Below: This photograph shows a throne at the palace of Knossos on Crete, the legendary home of King Minos.

Minos was the son of Zeus, ruler of the gods, and Europa, a beautiful Phoenician princess. Zeus lusted after Europa and transformed himself into a bull to carry the princess away to Crete. There, according to most versions of the story, she bore him three sons—Minos, Rhadamanthys, and Sarpedon—although Greek poet Homer (c. ninth–eighth century BCE) does not cite Sarpedon as Minos's brother. After Zeus left the island, Europa married the Cretan king Asterius, who raised the three boys as his own. When they were young men, all three of the brothers fell in love with Miletus, a semidivine son of Apollo. They quarreled over Miletus and, in some accounts, Minos expelled his brothers from the island forever.

With his brothers banished, Minos ascended the Cretan throne unchallenged on the death of Asterius. Still, he felt the need to demonstrate to his Cretan subjects that the gods wanted him to be king, so he prayed for a divine sign that would publicly acknowledge his right. Poseidon, god of the sea, answered Minos's prayer and sent a beautiful bull from out of the waves. Poseidon made Minos promise that once all the Cretans had recognized the significance of the bull, Minos was to sacrifice the animal to the sea god. However, when the bull appeared and Minos was universally proclaimed king, he ignored Poseidon's instructions. Some versions claim that he could not bring himself to kill the bull because the creature looked so majestic. Others say that the bull reminded him of the form Zeus took when he wooed Europa, and that he could not kill something that resembled his own father. Whatever the reason, instead of sacrificing Poseidon's bull, Minos killed

Below: This sculpture of a pair of bull horns is located at the palace of Knossos on Crete. Bulls featured prominently in Cretan religion.

Minoan Worship

Cretan, or Minoan, influence may be seen in many Greek myths. For example, ancient Greeks believed that in order to protect the infant Zeus from being devoured by his father, Cronus, his mother, Rhea, hid the divine baby in a cave on Mount Dicte in Crete, where he was raised by nymphs. Caves were of great significance to Minoans: within them they seem to have practiced a religious cult celebrating fertility gods. Numerous votive offerings have been found in such locations—these were usually in the form of domesticated animals such as sheep, goats, and bulls, but in one particular cave a large cache of turtles was excavated.

Minoans also worshiped their gods in sanctuaries and at altars on the tops of mountains. The altars, built in the form of stylized bull horns, marked the location of cave sanctuaries; the bull horns topped the peak sanctuary building as well. However, modern archaeologists have not yet been able to ascertain the exact forms of worship that took place in these isolated sacred sites.

Right: This Roman floor mosaic from the fourth century CE depicts Greek hero Theseus fighting the Minotaur in the Labyrinth.

the best bull from his own herd. This did not satisfy Poseidon. On the contrary, the sea god viewed Minos's failure as blasphemy, and he swore revenge.

Pasiphae and the Minotaur

Minos had married Pasiphae, a daughter of the sun god Helios, and made her his queen. Together they had four sons—Catreus, Deucalion, Glaucus, and Androgeos—and five daughters—Ariadne, Phaedra, Acacallis, Xenodice, and Euryale. Minos also had many illegitimate children. After years of enduring her husband's infidelities, Pasiphae concocted a potion that made Minos imagine that snakes and scorpions were coming out of his body whenever he made love to another woman.

Poseidon finally took his revenge on Minos by causing Pasiphae to fall helplessly in love with the bull from the sea. However, the animal did not reciprocate her affections. While Minos was abroad expanding his empire, Pasiphae summoned Daedalus, the court inventor, to devise a contraption that would enable her to make love with the bull. He built a hollow statue of a cow inside which Pasiphae could lie. When the bull saw the effigy in his pasture, he mistook it for a real cow and mounted it, thus impregnating the queen of Crete. The product of this union was a baby boy with a bull's head. Our primary source for the story of Pasiphae and the bull is *The Cretans*, a play credited to Greek dramatist Euripides (c. 486–c. 406 BCE). Now lost, the work is reputed to have had Pasiphae arguing that it must have been the gods who made her fall in love with the bull in order to punish Minos, and denying that it was as a result of anything she had done.

When Minos returned from his travels, he was so disgusted at the sight of the bull-headed infant that he commissioned Daedalus to create a home for it hidden deep beneath the royal palace. Daedalus built a massive, complex maze from which the monster was unable to escape because it could never find the exit. Named the Minotaur, the bull-headed creature lived on human flesh.

Events outside of Crete provided a gruesome supply of food for the beast. Minos's son Androgeos was a great athlete. He won the Panathenaic Games, which were held in Athens in honor of the goddess Athena, but was murdered shortly after his victory. In vengeance, Minos laid siege to Athens. Although he had a mighty army, he was unable to conquer the city. Minos prayed to his father for help. In response, Zeus sent a plague and famine to Athens.

The Athenians, desperate to find ways of ending their suffering, sought the advice of an oracle who told them that they should submit to whatever terms Minos demanded. In return for ending the siege, Minos required that a tribute of seven youths and seven girls be sent to Crete (either annually or every nine years) as food for the Minotaur. The tribute ended only when the Athenian hero Theseus killed the Minotaur and escaped from the Labyrinth with the help of Minos's daughter Ariadne.

Pursuit of Daedalus

Theseus was able to find his way out of the Labyrinth with the help of a plan devised by Daedalus. When Minos discovered the inventor's role in the death of the Minotaur, he threw Daedalus and his son, Icarus, into the Labyrinth.

Drawing Parallels

The story of Ariadne and Theseus is thought by some to parallel the rise of Athens and the fall of Crete. As Attica (a peninsula of mainland Greece) became the commercial and artistic center of the Mediterranean world, the old mother goddess–worshiping civilization of Crete became an increasing menace. When Theseus made his way to the heart of the Labyrinth and slew the Minotaur, metaphorically he murdered the ancient civilization that had ruled over the incipient democracy and its patriarchal culture. In the story of the escape of Theseus and Ariadne from Crete, he abandons the daughter of Minos on the island of Naxos. Some argue that Theseus's cruelty to Ariadne is a metaphor for the passing of the old tradition and the beginning of the new order of the sky god. Heedless of Ariadne's grief-stricken cries, Theseus left her weeping and sailed home alone. His punishment was that his return to Athens would cause his own father to commit suicide.

Ever the inventor, Daedalus fashioned two pairs of wings out of wax and feathers, one pair for himself and the other for Icarus. After escaping from the Labyrinth, the two flew high into the sky away from Crete. Yet only Daedalus reached safety. Icarus, ignoring his father's warnings, flew too close to the sun. The heat melted the wax in his wings, and the boy fell to his death. Daedalus eventually found refuge in Sicily at the court of King Cocalos.

Minos tries to capture Daedalus

Minos became obsessed with capturing Daedalus. He devised a cunning plan to flush the inventor out of hiding by appealing to his vanity. The king traveled the world offering a prize to anyone who could pass a thread through a spiral-shaped seashell, knowing that only Daedalus had the skill to accomplish such a feat. For years Minos traveled to all the major courts offering his challenge, but no one proved clever enough to solve it. Finally he reached Sicily and the court of Cocalos. Daedalus, in disguise, examined the seashell carefully and took it away with him. After only a few moments he returned, having threaded the shell. He had solved the puzzle by boring a hole in the closed end of the shell and tying a thread to an ant. He then made the ant walk through the shell, pulling the thread behind it.

Minos recognized Daedalus and demanded that Cocalos hand over the inventor. Reluctantly the Sicilian king agreed, but he would not do so until after a night's rest. Believing that his years of search were at an end, Minos decided to relax in a bath poured for him by the daughters of Cocalos. Unknown to Minos, the girls adored Daedalus and were not willing to let him be taken away. According to some versions of the story, the girls poured either boiling water or pitch over Minos, scalding him to death. In other accounts the girls conspired with Daedalus to run a pipe through the roof of the room in which Minos was bathing. The girls filled the pipe with boiling water and, while Minos was relaxing in his bath, they poured it on him.

In the afterlife Minos became one of three judges of souls in the underworld. Rhadamanthys, Minos's brother, was the judge of Europeans; Aeacus—another of Zeus's semidivine sons—presided over Asians; while Minos determined the fate of those whose lives had been most complicated or difficult to judge. The ancient Greeks believed that both good and bad deeds were repaid a hundredfold in the afterlife, so the judgment of Minos

Left: This Roman bas-relief carving shows King Minos (right) making an offering to the god Neptune (the Roman equivalent of Poseidon).

Above: The entrance to Knossos. This ancient palace on Crete was first excavated by English archaeologist Arthur Evans around 1900.

was a terrifying prospect to people who feared retribution for the wicked deeds they had performed during their time on earth.

Uncovering the real Crete

According to legend, King Minos made Crete a center of commerce in the eastern Mediterranean and received tribute from cities such as Athens as a sign of his hegemony. Although it is known that from around 3500 BCE to 1100 BCE Crete was indeed wealthy and powerful, no archaeological evidence has been found to prove the existence of a historical Cretan ruler named Minos. Nevertheless, when British archaeologist Arthur Evans (1851–1941) first excavated the palace of Knossos, he named the ancient Cretan civilization thus uncovered "Minoan" in honor of the mythical king.

Minoan Art

Minoan art of the Bronze Age (which started around 3000 BCE) reveals a culture that was rich in the pleasures of the senses. The severe, abstract art of Neolithic Crete gave way about 2400–2300 BCE to curves, spirals, and meanders. These designs are reminiscent of the labyrinth at Knossos. Some Cretan artistic conventions were clearly borrowed from the culture of Egypt. Cretan figures, however, suggest the idea of a subject, such as the cat, while Egyptian figures capture the details. The paintings of bulls and bull dancers are the most evocative works of Minoan art. They reflect a fascination with the bull as a figure of fertility and power, combining both feminine and masculine divine powers. In the legends of Minos, the labyrinth and the bull are recurrent themes. Minos thus becomes the representative and champion of an ancient culture that was threatened by the rise of the Greeks and their maritime empire.

Above: This illustration by French artist Gustave Doré (1832–1883) shows Minos (foreground) judging souls in the underworld.

On the walls of the palace of Knossos there are frescoes depicting festivals, domestic parties, and nature scenes. It appears that the Minoans, like the ancient Etruscans of Italy, lived in a hedonistic society in which pleasure and freedom were of great importance. Although little is known of the Minoan social structure, it is thought that men and women had similar rights, and that wives were not mere subjects of their husbands. By 1500 BCE, Greek-speaking Mycenaeans began to settle the island, and Minoan culture was adapted and later replaced.

Cataclysmic event

One explanation historians cite for the downfall of the Minoan culture is a series of earthquakes followed by the largest recorded volcanic eruption on the island of Thera, to the north of Crete. It is known that Thera was once a thriving stopover port on the busy shipping route between Crete and Athens. The fact that archaeologists have found no evidence of human remains there has led them to conclude that the earthquakes must have forced the island's inhabitants to leave in a great hurry just before the catastrophe. The eruption is thought to have sent a tidal wave to the north coast of Crete, and to have caused a cloud of ash to reach as far as the easternmost parts of the Mediterranean. The tidal wave and ash cloud would have had a devastating impact on Minoan culture. The nature of Thera's fate is often associated with the myth surrounding the lost city of Atlantis. Some time later the island was repopulated by non-Minoan peoples.

BARBARA GARDNER

Bibliography

Farnaux, Alexandre, and David J. Baker, trans. *Knossos: Searching for the Legendary Palace of King Minos*. New York: Harry N. Abrams, 1996.

Macgillivray, Joseph Alexander. *Minotaur: Sir Arthur Evans and the Archaeology of the Minoan Myth*. New York: Hill and Wang, 2000.

SEE ALSO: Ariadne; Crete; Daedalus; Deucalion; Europa; Helios; Icarus; Pasiphae; Poseidon; Theseus; Zeus.

MITHRAISM

Mithraism was originally the worship of the god Mithra in Persia (modern-day Iran) before the time of the religious reformer Zoroaster (c. 600 BCE). The Persian Mithra was the god of the sun, justice, and war. Later, during the second and third centuries CE, the Romans adopted Mithra and changed his name to Mithras. He was the favorite god of soldiers.

Our knowledge of Mithraism, like that of many other ancient religions, is incomplete because of the dearth of religious texts about the belief system. The Roman period, when Mithraism became the single most important rival of Christianity, has yielded no Mithraic holy book. The most detailed descriptions of Mithras (or Mithra) are found in the religious texts of ancient India and Persia, which preceded the Roman worship of Mithras by many centuries. The Roman evidence for Mithras, on the other hand, consists chiefly of sculptures. As the Belgian expert on Mithras, Franz Cumont (1868–1947), pointed out, our knowledge of Mithraism may thus be compared to what we would know of Christianity if we had only the Old Testament and the paintings, sculptures, and statues in medieval churches at our disposal.

Mithras was originally an Indo-Iranian god known as Mithra. He was said to have been born miraculously from a rock. The earliest appearance of his name occurs in a peace treaty from around 1350 BCE between Suppiluliumas, king of the Hittites, and Kurtiwaza

Below: The Hindu god Varuna, depicted riding a makara or sea monster. The fact that Varuna's name was sometimes invoked with that of Mithra shows that Mithraism was of Indo-Iranian origin.

(or Mattiwaza), king of the Mitanni. This document, written in cuneiform (a writing system that used wedge-shaped characters), was found in 1907 in the royal archives of Hattushash (Bogazköy), the ancient Hittite capital, in modern Turkey. In the document Mithra is invoked together with several other gods—Indra, Varuna, and the Nasatyanna—as a protector of the treaty. Guarding agreements between people may have been one of the original functions of the god. In the language of the pre-Hindu Vedic texts from India, the word *mitra* means "friendship" or "contract," while in Avestan, the ancient language of Persia, *mithra* has a similar meaning.

In the Indian Rig Veda, a collection of sacred hymns to the Vedic gods, Mithra (or, more accurately, Mitra) is often paired with the deity Varuna, and only one hymn is dedicated to Mithra alone. The hymns to Mithra as Varuna probably date from the 14th century BCE. In them, Mithra is described as the god "who brings people together." He is a benevolent deity who is differentiated from the other gods by his unshakable sense of honor. For example, when the other gods express their wish to murder Soma, the god of life, in order that they may enjoy immortality, Mithra at first refuses to join them. Only when he realizes that the death of Soma is inevitable does he agree.

Mithra in Persia

In the Persian Avestan literature, Mithra becomes an immensely popular figure. He fights at the side of the good gods, who are led by the great deity of light, Ahura Mazda. Their chief adversary is Angra Mainyu, the lord of evil. Initially in the *Avesta*, the holy scriptures of the religious reformer Zoroaster, Mithra plays a secondary role to Ahura Mazda. Later, however, his influence increases again, and in one *yasht*, or "hymn," dedicated to Mithra, he is proclaimed to be as worthy of worship and prayer as Ahura Mazda.

It was in Persia that Mithra was first thought of as a god of light. A *yasht* dating from the reign of Persian king Cyrus the Great (c. 585–c. 529 BCE) describes Mithra as the "god of the dawn that rises over Mount Hara and embraces in his gaze the whole country of the Aryans." The tomb of Cyrus at Pasargadae (the ancient capital of Persia, in modern Iran) has on its pediment a rosette that may have been carved to represent the sun as a symbol of Mithra. If this interpretation is correct, it would seem that the great king of the Persians endorsed the worship of Mithra as the god of light.

The worship of Mithra survived the promotion of Zoroastrianism under the Persian king Darius I (ruled 522–486 BCE) and his successors. It also survived the fall of the Persian Empire when it was conquered by Alexander the Great (356–323 BCE) and even the turbulent times of rapid cultural change following Alexander's death. Mithra was especially popular with the rulers of Armenia, Cappadocia, Pontus, and Commagene—regions where the cult had been introduced during the Persian occupation of western Asia. Several kings of Pontus were even named Mithradates, meaning "given by Mithra," starting with Mithradates I (ruled 302–266 BCE). In Commagene, in eastern Turkey, a famous relief sculpture at Nimrud Dagh depicts King Antiochus I of Commagene (ruled 62–34 BCE) shaking hands with Mithra, implying that he had a privileged relationship with a powerful god and was, therefore, a powerful king.

As the worship of Mithra spread westward, his name began to be rendered as "Mithras." In Tarsus, the capital of Cilicia (a region in what is now southern Turkey), the worship of Mithras appears to have blended with local worship of the Greek hero Perseus, famous for killing the Gorgon Medusa and rescuing the princess Andromeda.

Some new elements in the iconography of Mithras, most notably the Phrygian hat (a brimless cap with a curled top), may have been taken from portrayals of Perseus. Distinctive astrological ideas also became incorporated into Mithraic worship, possibly from Stoic philosophy, a Greek school of philosophy that accepted certain astrological principles and was just at the height of its influence in Tarsus. It was in this same period and place that the worship of Mithras was transformed into a mystery cult, a religion that revolves around secret ceremonies.

Below: The tomb of Cyrus the Great at Pasargadae. The triangular pediment or gable has a carved rosette that is thought to represent the sun, and therefore perhaps to symbolize Mithras.

Iconography and Myth

The Romans usually depicted Mithras as a young, beardless man in Persian clothes (long trousers, a loose shirt, and a short cloak), wearing a Phrygian hat (a brimless cap with a curled top). Sometimes he is accompanied by his two smaller but similarly attired assistants, the torchbearers Cautes and Cautopates.

Complete stories of Mithras's early life are virtually nonexistent, but fragments of text and visual representations suggest that he had no parents and it was believed that he was born miraculously from a rock. He was responsible for the workings of the cosmos, so he was also responsible for the seasons and the crops.

Mithras is often depicted killing a bull, a representation of the following myth. At one time the proper balance of the universe was threatened by a (cosmic) bull, who was draining all the life-giving moisture from the moon. Mithras had to kill the animal but took no pleasure in the act, as is clear from the way he turns his head away in representations of the scene. He killed the animal with a swift thrust of a dagger to the neck. However, the killing of the bull was a miraculous event. Ears of corn shot from the tail of the dying bull, and, thanks to Mithras, the natural order was restored. The death of the animal brought a renewal of the earth and of life. A small dog and a serpent rushed to the scene to partake of the life-giving blood, while a scorpion attacked the bull's genitals.

This story is reminiscent of that of the earlier god of life, Soma, who had to die in order to give eternal life to the other gods.

Mithras and the Romans

According to Greek writer Plutarch (c. 46–120 CE), the Romans first came into contact with the mystery cult of Mithras in 67 BCE through contacts with Cilician pirates. The valiant young god had a particular attraction for Roman soldiers, from the rank and file all the way up to the legion commanders. The worship of Mithras spread throughout the Roman Empire via the military camps. Several Roman emperors are known to have worshiped Mithras. They include Commodus (ruled 180–192 CE), Septimius Severus (ruled 193–211 CE), Caracalla (ruled 211–217 CE), and Geta (ruled 209–212 CE). The Mithras cult flourished under these and subsequent emperors.

Evidence for the worship of Mithras has been discovered in the form of dedications and *mithraea* (Mithras sanctuaries) in Syria, Numidia (an ancient kingdom in North Africa), Carthage (a city in North Africa), Morocco, Gaul (France and Belgium), Britain, and all along the Roman Empire's frontier. The most discoveries have been made in the German outposts and in the provinces

Below: This bas-relief of the second century CE shows a banquet held by worshipers of Mithras in honor of their god.

Above: This photograph shows part of the interior of the Temple of Mithras at the Circus Maximus in Rome.

surrounding the Danube River, which flows through central and southern Europe. Along the Roman frontier the founding of new *mithraea* was usually connected with Roman army camps.

Places of worship

In addition to Mithraic worship by Roman soldiers along the frontiers, Mithras was also immensely popular in port towns, such as Ostia, the port of Rome. Merchants and other sailors in port towns regarded him as the protector of seafaring and trade.

In Ostia 16 places have thus far been identified as *mithraea*: 14 within the old city and two in the Palazzo Imperiale outside the city. The earliest date from the second century CE, and the latest from the fourth century CE. Their distribution over the city is remarkably even, which

Secret Place of Worship

The central room of a *mithraeum* was usually a small, rectangular space located on ground level, often in the back of a private home. On either side of a central aisle were high oblong podiums, on which the celebrants lay together to enjoy a communal meal. The shape of the room often resembled that of a cave or crypt. An altar and a depiction of Mithras killing a bull were generally placed at the end of the aisle, close to the rear wall. In this way, the attention of anyone entering would immediately be drawn to the scene.

Although the central room was often small, the overall size of a *mithraeum*, including annexes, could vary considerably. The maximum capacity was about 20 men (women were excluded) and hardly ever more than 40, indicating that the worshipers of Mithras preferred to keep their cult groups small. When a *mithraeum* had reached its maximum capacity, the worshipers would simply build a new one.

The Mithraeum of Felicissimus

In 1940, during major excavations in Ostia (the port of Rome, Italy), an extraordinary mosaic was uncovered in a room on the southern edge of the city. The mosaic depicts the seven grades of initiation into the mysteries of Mithras, of which previously only the names were known. At the head of the seven tableaux is an inscription that says "Felicissimus dedicated this in accordance with a vow." From this inscription, the room takes its modern name, the Mithraeum of Felicissimus.

Since the original entrance to the room had been walled up, the sanctuary could be accessed only through an adjoining room. By the entrance were a small basin and a few plain mosaics. The floor of the main aisle was decorated with a symbolic representation of the seven grades of initiation, which were connected with the seven so-called planets.

The order of the planets is unique to the Mithras cult. There were two standard orders of the planets in antiquity. The first, the Chaldean order, arranged the celestial bodies on the basis of their supposed distance from the earth (from farthest to closest): Saturn, Jupiter, Mars, Sun, Venus, Mercury, Moon. The other order, which is still used for the days of the week, was formed by starting with Saturn and skipping two planets every time: Saturn, Sun, Moon, Mars, Mercury, Jupiter, Venus. The order of the planets in the Mithras cult was an amalgamation of the two sequences. The highest grade was connected to the most important planet, Saturn.

INITIATE GRADE	PLANET	SYMBOLS
Pater (Father)	Saturn	sickle, Phrygian hat, staff, bowl
Heliodromus (Sun-runner)	Sun	whip, sun crown, torch
Perses (Persian)	Moon	moon, sickle, scythe or plow, star
Leo (Lion)	Jupiter	lightning, rattle, fire shovel
Miles (Soldier)	Mars	spear, helmet, knapsack
Nymphus (Newlywed)	Venus	diadem, lamp
Corax (Raven)	Mercury	raven, cup, Mercury's staff

Above: This Roman sculpture of Mithras depicts the god's miraculous birth from a rock.

has led historians to assume that Romans took the location of existing *mithraea* into account when building a new *mithraeum*. In other places *mithraea* were often built underground, presumably so that they would resemble the cave in which Mithras was said to be born from the rock. In Ostia the *mithraea* were not (or were only partially) underground because of the high ground water level and the flooding of the Tiber River in winter. None of the *mithraea* of Ostia is situated directly on a main road or on a square. They were in secluded places, which added to the secretive character of the cult.

Despite its great popularity throughout the empire among all types of people, Mithraism was never an official state cult. *Mithraea* were never built in *loca publica* (public spaces), nor were there any holidays connected with the god. This evidence supports the view that Mithraism was a distinctly private religion.

Worship and ritual

As a mystery cult, Mithraism revolved around secret ritual. The initiates, known as the *mystai*, were the only people to know about the workings of the cult. Mithraic groups were exclusive, and only men were allowed to participate. The initiates would share dinner together, perhaps daily. Because most *mithraea* were small and unsuitable for bloody sacrifices, it is likely that the meat for the meal came from a butcher in most instances, not from a sacrificial animal that was killed inside the *mithraeum*.

The initiates had to pass through seven grades of initiation, from Corax to Pater (see box, opposite). Each of these grades was connected with one of the seven "planets" (the five planets that were known at the time, plus the sun and the moon). It is likely that an initiate had to undergo increasingly difficult ritual tests, or ordeals, to be accepted to the higher grades.

Origen's account

Origen (c. 185–254 CE), a writer and mystic of the early Christian church, comments on the role of the stars and planets in Mithraism: "Plato taught that, in order to descend from heaven to earth and to ascend from earth to heaven, the souls pass across the planets. The Persians represented the same idea in their mysteries of Mithras. They have a symbol that represents the two movements taking place in heaven, that is, the movement of the fixed stars and that of the planets, and another one to figure the journey of the soul across the heavenly bodies. This latter symbol is a tall ladder with seven gates and an eighth at the top. The first gate is made of lead, the second of tin, the third of copper, the fourth of iron, the fifth of an alloy, the sixth of silver, and the seventh of gold."

The decline of Mithraism

The decline of the worship of Mithras in Rome is closely related to the rise of another religion—Christianity. In 307 former emperor Diocletian, emperor Galerius, and future emperor Licinius restored a *mithraeum* at Carnuntum in Upper Pannonia (modern Austria), designating Mithras *fautor imperii sui* (protector of imperial power). Only a few years later, however, Emperor Constantine (c. 280–337 CE) defeated his opponent Maxentius in the Battle of Milvian Bridge (312 CE) and declared that he had triumphed under the sign of Christ. Christianity then became the official state religion of Rome, replacing the older religions.

Just as Christianity had been repressed by Galerius and Diocletian, Mithraism was now officially repressed by the new regime. Mithraic worshipers were no longer allowed to have their communal meals, and meetings between initiates were broken up. Over the course of time many *mithraea* were deliberately destroyed by zealous Christians, the statues destroyed or defaced, and the paintings attacked with knives. The famous *mithraeum* that today is sited

Right: The veneration of snakes was an important part of Mithraism. This Greco-Roman marble statue of the second century BCE was found in a temple to the god at Tomi, near Constanta, Romania.

A Cosmological Interpretation of the Bull-killing Scene

Depictions of Mithras killing the cosmic bull usually contain pictures of the animals of the following constellations: Taurus (bull), Canis minor (dog), Hydra (serpent), Corvus (raven), and Scorpius (scorpion). Occasionally, a lion for the constellation Leo and a cup or jar for Aquarius are also depicted.

A line drawn through the constellations that correspond to the animals of the bull-killing scene coincides exactly with the location of the celestial equator between 4000 and 2000 BCE. The celestial equator is an imaginary line that describes the earth's equator projected onto the stars. Because the earth's axis shifts constantly, the earth's equator—and hence also the celestial equator—also shifts steadily in relation to the ecliptic. The ecliptic is the line along which the sun appears to move through the sky every year because of the earth's rotation around the sun. (It is also the line on which the signs of the zodiac are located.) The ecliptic and the celestial equator intersect twice a year when day and night have the same length: the equinoxes. The shifting of the earth's axis results in a corresponding shift of the equinoxes on the ecliptic. This is known as the precession of the equinoxes.

The equinoxes were held to be of sacred importance by the worshipers of Mithras. The spring equinox was especially sacred, since it marked the anniversary of the killing of the bull. The bull-killing scene in its turn harks back to the time when the spring equinox was in Taurus, 4000–2000 BCE.

Below: This bas-relief of the second century CE shows Mithras killing a bull. Note the serpent (bottom left).

under the San Clemente church in Rome was raided several times. The altar, which was damaged in the first of these assaults, shows signs of having been repaired by members of the community, who were finally forced to abandon their sanctuary. By erecting a church over the old *mithraeum*, the Christians demonstrated their victory over Mithraism.

FEYO SCHUDDEBOOM

Bibliography

Clauss, Manfred, and Richard Gordon, trans. *The Roman Cult of Mithras: The God and His Mysteries.* New York: Routledge, 2001.

Ulansey, David. *The Origins of the Mithraic Mysteries: Cosmology and Salvation in the Ancient World.* New York: Oxford University Press, 1991.

SEE ALSO: Calendar; Creation Myths; Iran; Mystery Cults; Perseus; Rome; Stars.

MNEMOSYNE

In Greek myth, Mnemosyne was the personification of memory. She played a personal role in only one story, that of her affair with Zeus, king of the gods, which produced nine offspring—the Muses, the goddesses of the arts. However, Mnemosyne's symbolic significance ensured that she was an important member of the Greek pantheon, since people recognized that storytelling and recorded history were impossible without memory.

Mnemosyne was one of the Titans, the 12 divine beings born from the union between Gaia (earth) and Uranus (sky). Some of the Titans personified aspects of the natural world—Oceanus (the world river), Hyperion (the sun), and Phoebe (the moon). Others represented abstract ideas. Mnemosyne belonged to the latter category, as did her sister Themis (justice), and—possibly, since the sources are not entirely clear—Coeus (intelligence) and Theia (sight).

Birth of the Muses

Unlike monotheists, who believe that creation was the action of a single god, ancient Greeks believed that the world was generated by a series of divine matings. Zeus, who became king of the gods after the Olympian deities defeated the Titans, fathered numerous divine beings through his affairs with a succession of female Titans, goddesses, and nymphs. He also sired many legendary heroes and demigods through a string of liaisons with mortal women. According to one story, after the Olympians defeated the Titans, they asked Zeus to create deities who would help them to celebrate their victory. In response to their request, Zeus went from Mount Olympus to nearby Pieria, where he disguised himself as a shepherd and seduced Mnemosyne. The couple slept together for nine consecutive nights. The result of their union was the birth of nine female children. These were the Muses, each of whom held sway over one particular artistic

Below: The exterior of this sarcophagus, dated about 150 CE, is decorated with bas-reliefs of the Muses, the nine daughters of Mnemosyne.

Memory, Writing, and Forgetfulness

Are books essential for culture and learning? We are brought up to believe that they are, but Greek philosopher Plato questioned this assumption. In his book *Phaedrus* he acknowledged the importance of memory for speech and intellect, but doubted the benefit of writing to memory. *Phaedrus* contains an imaginary conversation between two Egyptian deities, Thamus, the chief god, and Theuth, a god of inventions. In the book, Theuth invents writing and shows it to Thamus, suggesting that the skill should be taught to all Egyptians. Thamus, however, doubts Theuth's assertion that writing will make people wiser and improve their memories. The chief god fears that writing will encourage forgetfulness, since people would no longer use their memory to recall names, events, and ideas, but would instead look things up in books. "You offer your pupils the appearance of wisdom, not true wisdom," Thamus says, "for they will read many things without instruction … when for the most part they are ignorant."

form: Calliope (epic poetry), Clio (history), Euterpe (flute playing), Erato (lyric poetry), Melpomene (tragedy), Thalia (comedy), Terpsichore (dancing), Polymnia (music), and Urania (astronomy).

Greek geographer Pausanias (143–176 CE) gives a different account of the origins of the Muses. According to him, the people of Sicyon in the northern Peloponnese believed that there were only three Muses, each of whom had responsibility for a different aspect of art in performance: Melete was the goddess of practice, Mneme of memory, and Aeode of song. Pausanias further related that it was a man named Pierus, from Macedonia, to the north of Greece, who established belief in nine such goddesses. Pausanias is the only source of this alternative version, and it is likely that for most Greeks the Muses were always nine in number.

Abstract concept

Except for the story of the birth of the Muses, the character of Mnemosyne does not really figure in Greek mythology. This is perhaps unsurprising, since she was the personification of an abstract quality. Nevertheless, ancient writers occasionally described Mnemosyne's physical appearance. One Greek poet, Hesiod (fl. 800 BCE), wrote that she had "beautiful hair"; another, Pindar (c. 522–c. 438 BCE), described her as "golden-robed." A surviving fragment of poetry by Alcman, a Spartan of the

seventh century BCE, refers to Mnemosyne's big eyes, and this has been taken as a reference to the fact that memory allows people to "see" their past.

Although Mnemosyne had no other role than mother of the Muses, ancient Greeks still afforded the female Titan much significance. They believed that she was present in the recollection of every story told, since all narrators need memory to tell their tales. This was particularly true in oral cultures. By the ninth and eighth centuries BCE, writers such as Homer had begun to record stories by writing them down, but many people could still neither read nor write, so they relied on the tradition of oral storytelling to learn about gods and heroes.

Many sources reflect the symbolic importance of Mnemosyne, who not only personified memory, but also represented everything that memory made possible. An orphic hymn—from an undated collection of ancient Greek poems used by cult followers of the mythical musician Orpheus—describes how Mnemosyne freed the human mind from oblivion and, as a result, represented the joining of the soul with the intellect. In *Critias*—the title of which refers to one of the characters who take part in a series of dialogues—Greek philosopher Plato (c. 428–c. 348 BCE) discusses Mnemosyne's role in human intelligence. Critias explains that it is only because of his capacity to remember information and past events that he can participate in rational argument.

Language and history

Elsewhere in the work of Plato, Critias goes even further, suggesting that Mnemosyne played a major part in the development of human speech. This role was elaborated by Greek historian Diodorus Siculus (90–21 BCE), according to whom Mnemosyne gave humans the capacity to name and remember everything they saw and felt, which therefore allowed them to hold conversations with each other. Diodorus did, however, acknowledge that not everyone assigned such a role to Mnemosyne. He suggested that some people believed the power of language was a gift to humans from Hermes, divine messenger and god of eloquence. Another source, the undated "Homeric Hymn to Hermes," establishes a connection between the two deities. The hymn relates that Hermes honored Mnemosyne and was one of her followers.

The importance of Mnemosyne reflects that of the mental capacity she represents. Memory is widely regarded

Right: This painting of Mnemosyne is by English artist Frederick Leighton (1830–1896).

Left: This illustration depicts the oracle of Trophonius, which was associated with rites venerating Mnemosyne. Traditionally bees were reared there.

to history with the lines: "Holy Memory, reveal/the glories of yore:/how Spartans and Athenians/won the Persian war." This is a reference to the series of wars between the Greek states and Persia between 492 and 449 BCE.

Ancient Greeks believed that the Muses inspired the writing and performance of songs that honored famous events and noble deeds. Pindar wrote that, if people were successful, they would hope that the Muses would see to it that their success was recorded in song. Like their mother, the Muses—whose name in Greek means "remembrances"—were regarded as patronesses of memory.

Honoring Mnemosyne

Pausanias, in his travels around Greece in the second century CE, observed images of Mnemosyne and the Muses on the altar of Athena, goddess of arts and war, at Tegea in Arcadia, a mountainous region in the central Peloponnese. This was not the only example of Greeks honoring the female Titan: in his biography of the first-century CE philosopher Apollonius of Tyana, Philostratus (c. 170–c. 245 CE) recounted how Apollonius would chant a hymn to Mnemosyne. The hymn declared that, while everything is worn away by time, time itself does not age because of memory.

Pausanias also told of a ritual in honor of Mnemosyne that was held at the oracle of Trophonius in Lebadea, a town of Boeotia in east-central Greece. Anyone who wished to consult the oracle was taken by priests to two water fountains. Petitioners drank from the first fountain, which contained the waters of Lethe (Forgetfulness); thereafter they drank from the second, which contained the waters of Mnemosyne. They then consulted the oracle itself, and when they had finished they sat on a seat known as the chair of Mnemosyne, where the priests asked them to tell all that they had seen or learned.

KARELISA HARTIGAN

Bibliography

Bulfinch, Thomas. *Bulfinch's Mythology.* New York: Modern Library, 1998.
Pausanias, and Peter Levi, trans. *Guide to Greece.* New York: Viking Press, 1984.
Plato, and James H. Nichols, Jr., trans. *Gorgias and Phaedrus.* Ithaca, NY: Cornell University Press, 1998.

SEE ALSO: Athena; Gaia; Hermes; Muses; Orpheus; Titans; Uranus; Zeus.

as the foundation of everything that distinguishes humans from animals. It enables people to know who and what they are, and to retain that information. It is important at all times and in all cultures, but it was of particular significance in the ancient world, before scribes began to create and reproduce manuscripts. Memory remained crucial to the transmission of knowledge until the invention of the printing press in the 15th century CE. Henceforth, authors needed to remember information only until they had written it down.

Although memory is no longer so important to the survival and transmission of knowledge, it remains vital to human life. One of the ways in which people commit information to memory is with the aid of mnemonics—systems designed to assist or improve memory. Such aids—still important to modern people—were indispensable to ancient Greeks. Oral poetry was common in ancient Greek life; wandering bards and storytellers were able to entertain the Greek public using mnemonics to string together long recitals of tales they had learned or history they had experienced. In *Lysistrata*, Greek dramatist Aristophanes (c. 450–c. 388 BCE) invoked Mnemosyne's importance

MOMOS

In Greek mythology Momos was the personification of blame, and was associated with similar phenomena such as criticism, scorn, mockery, and ridicule. Momos was one of the earliest beings created. His sole parent was Nyx (or Night), herself a child of Chaos, the earliest entity in the creation of the cosmos.

Momos had several brothers and sisters; they included a number of unpleasant and grim figures such as Moros (Dissolution), Apate (Deceit), Nemesis (Retribution), Thanatos (Death), Oizus (Pain), Eris (Discord), and the Keres (Doom). Night created these offspring herself, without the help of any male consort. Momos was thus a primal entity that came into being very early in the history of creation, at the same time as the Titans, the Cyclopes, and the Hecatoncheires (Hundred-Handed Ones). The idea that a quality as negative as unrelenting sarcastic criticism is a fundamental component of reality reflects a characteristically Greek view of the world.

Momos and the Trojan War

In his poem the *Cypria*, Greek poet Stasinos (seventh century BCE) wrote that Momos played a key role in the early history of human affairs. Earth (Gaia) was weighed down by the overpopulation of the human race. To make matters worse, men and women were also insolent and disrespectful in their behavior toward the gods. Gaia complained to Zeus about her burden. The king of the gods considered using natural phenomena (such as thunderbolts, floods, or earthquakes) to relieve Gaia. However, Momos advised that the best way to bring about a reduction in population would be to use human beings' natural proclivity to fight one another. To prompt a great

Below: This illustration from a sixth-century-BCE drinking cup shows a scene from the Trojan War, a conflict that was partially instigated by Momos.

war Zeus would have to do two things: marry the sea nymph Thetis to a mortal, and father a daughter, Helen. Zeus accepted Momos's advice. At the wedding of Peleus and Thetis, Momos's sister Eris, who had not been invited, threw a golden apple into the midst of the guests, so setting into motion the chain of events that would lead to the Trojan War.

Below: This Greek statue from the first century BCE depicts Aphrodite (left, holding the squeaking sandal) with Cupid (center) and Pan. Although Aphrodite embodied physical perfection, Momos was still able to find fault with her.

The niggling, griping character of Momos is well illustrated in a traditional fable attributed to legendary Greek writer Aesop. Momos, who mixed with the gods on Olympus, was once called upon to judge the creations of three of them: Zeus, Prometheus, and Athena. Zeus had created the bull, Prometheus man, and Athena the house. Momos spitefully criticized their work. He argued that the bull should have its eyes above its horns, so that it could see where it was striking; man should have his heart hanging outside his body, so that his intentions would be apparent to everyone and the wicked would not be able to get away with things; and the house should be on wheels, so that people could easily move away if they had a bad neighbor. The incident annoyed Zeus so much that he expelled Momos from Olympus.

Momos became an emblem of continuous, insistent dissatisfaction, no matter what the circumstances. For example, he was so unable to resist being critical that he even found fault with Aphrodite, who was seen as a paragon of physical perfection. Momos agreed that although he could see nothing else wrong with the goddess, he did find it very irritating that her sandal squeaked.

Momos was often linked to the idea of Phthonas (Envy), especially when it was contrasted with reasonable appreciation or praise. For this reason Momos entered the language of literary debate. When their work was attacked, ancient Greek writers would often describe their critics as "children of Momos." In later writings, the term *momos* came to mean a defect or an immoral and reprehensible act of behavior that could invite reproach.

Momos experienced something of a revival in the mid-15th century when Italian mathematician, writer, and painter Leon Battista Alberti (1404–1472) wrote the fictional work *Momus* (an alternative spelling of *Momos*). It resurrected the mythical figure to satirize numerous aspects of contemporary society. In the late 16th century, poet Thomas Lodge the Younger (1558–1625) wrote the collection of poems *A Fig for Momus*.

ANTHONY BULLOCH

Bibliography

Alberti, Leon Battista, and Virginia Brown, ed. *Momus*. Cambridge, MA: Harvard University Press, 2003.
Hesiod, and M. L. West, trans. *Theogony; and Works and Days*. New York: Oxford University Press, 1999.

SEE ALSO: Aphrodite; Helen; Paris; Prometheus; Zeus.

MONOTHEISM

Monotheism is belief in one god. The term stands in contrast to atheism, belief in no god, and to polytheism, belief in many gods. Unlike pantheism, the belief that god is inseparable from the world, monotheism holds that god is transcendent, or outside the world. Monotheism also differs from deism, the belief that god has withdrawn from the world, because it maintains that god is immanent, or active in it.

Below: A religious Hindu practices yoga, which brings the soul into contact with Brahman.

Commentators recognize two types of monotheism, which they describe as ethical and intellectual, although the two are often closely related. In ethical monotheism the one god exists because believers feel the need to worship only one entity. In intellectual monotheism the existence of one god is the logical outcome of questions about how the world was created, which lead back to the conclusion that one thing existed before all others.

The god of monotheism is generally not an impersonal, abstract entity but one that has human traits and often can be imagined as having power, wisdom, and usually love. Although his infinite capacities are too great to be understood, he can be approached in prayer.

Today the world's most popular monotheistic religions are Judaism, Christianity, and Islam. All three creeds have become widespread because they have provided emotionally satisfying answers to many of humanity's

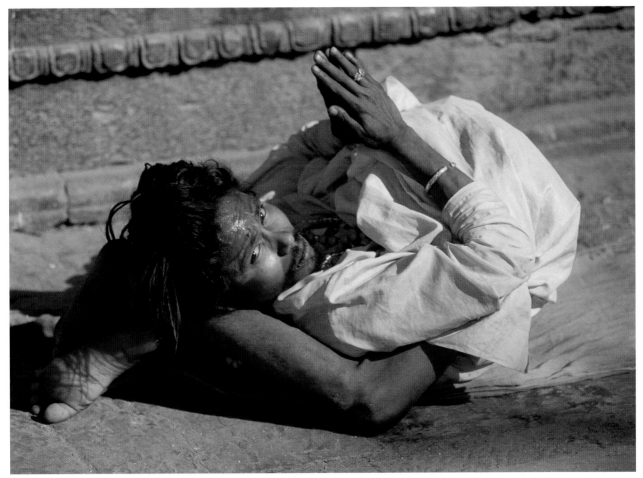

Oneness and the Trinity

As far as is known, the earliest Christians were strict monotheists—they believed in what has become known as the concept of Oneness. The idea of the Holy Trinity—God the Father, God the Son, and God the Holy Spirit (or Holy Ghost)—did not emerge until all 12 of Jesus Christ's disciples had died, thus bringing to an end the period known as the Apostolic Age. The most prominent post-apostolic church leaders were Hermas, Clement of Rome, Polycarp, and Ignatius. Their ministries spanned the period from about 90 to 140 CE. None referred to the existence of a Trinity.

Saint Irenaeus (c. 120–c. 200 CE), a Greek prelate, described Jesus as God manifested in flesh. This may have been no more than a metaphor for the diverse roles of the creator. Even if Irenaeus meant it literally, it is unlikely that he regarded this fission as anything more than a temporary measure: once Jesus had rejoined God in Heaven, Oneness would be restored.

The words of Irenaeus gave rise to the dogma of the Holy Trinity. It soon became widespread because it satisfied the perceived need to emphasize that Jesus was more than just a great teacher who had been adopted by God, but that he was actually the son of the Almighty. The third member of the Trinity, the Holy Spirit, was the emanation from which worshipers drew their faith.

Difficulties soon emerged in formulating and understanding the concept of the Trinity. Different interpretations led early to numerous controversies such as those over subordinationism (the teaching that the Son is subordinate to the Father and the Holy Spirit to both) and modalism (the idea that the three modes are transitory). The disputes were eventually settled by the Christian Councils of Nicaea (325) and Constantinople (381), which affirmed that the Trinity was a Oneness and expressly rejected all other doctrines.

Above: This 19th-century oil painting depicts the departure of Abraham from Ur, where some Hebrews first started worshiping a single deity.

Above: Fortifications around the monastery of Saint Katarina in Sinai, Egypt, bear witness to historic tensions between Christianity and Islam, which are both exclusive monotheisms.

abiding questions about the meaning of existence. However, they have also left their followers with problematic issues to address. Having postulated a supreme deity who is almighty, all knowing, and everywhere, and whose principal concern is the welfare of humans, they have found it hard to explain how evil, pain, and suffering fit into his—the monotheistic religions traditionally see god as being male—great scheme of things. Some Christian writers—notably English author John Milton (1608–1674) in his epic poem *Paradise Lost*—tried to resolve the contradiction by suggesting that god had given humans and angels "free will." However, this explanation begs the question of why, if the deity was good and could foresee everything, he did not act to prevent misfortune. The answer usually comes through what is termed a leap of faith: believers must accept that god's goodness surpasses human understanding.

Monotheism before the Old Testament

The three most popular monotheisms are all based on the Old Testament of the Bible. Jews, Christians, and Muslims traditionally believe that the existence of only one god was revealed by God to Adam, the first human, in the Garden of Eden. This story is recounted in Genesis, the first book of the Bible. Some scholars believe that Old Testament

monotheism may itself have roots in ancient Egypt, specifically the attempt by the pharaoh Amenhotep IV (ruled 1379–1362 BCE) to replace the pantheon of Egyptian deities with the sun god Aton. Amenhotep, who renamed himself Akhenaton ("Follower of Aton"), instituted the sole worship of Aton, whom he declared had created every aspect of life. However, this attempt at establishing monotheism proved shortlived. Popular belief in Aton never caught on—partially because there were no myths surrounding the god to appeal to ordinary people— and after Amenhotep's death, worship of the god declined.

Polytheistic Jews?

According to tradition, the earliest Jews lived in Ur, an ancient city near the mouth of the Tigris and Euphrates rivers in Mesopotamia (part of modern Iraq), until their patriarch Abraham led them to the land of Canaan (modern Palestine). The range of gods and goddesses worshiped by Ur's inhabitants left a lasting impression on Jewish culture. Modern archaeologists have discovered statues of the goddess Ashtoreth, who is equivalent to the Babylonian goddess Ishtar, in the women's quarters of a rabbi's home in Israel. The quarters in which the statues were found dated from the early years of the first century CE. Whoever lived there would have been in defiance of an edict that outlawed the worship of any god other than Yahweh, the supreme being of monotheistic Judaism.

Judaism, Christianity, Islam, and Zoroastrianism

In both Judaism and Islam, god is the creator and all-powerful ruler of the universe. He has no rivals or subordinate deities. He is also just and loving to people who trust him and follow his strict moral code: He will reward them for their obedience by saving them from sin and death. Those who are disrespectful or who deny him will be damned for eternity. Christianity is largely the same, except that it has adopted the doctrine of the Trinity—"God the Father, God the Son, and God the Holy Spirit" (see box, page 906). Yet in practice this, too, is monotheism:

there are not three Christian gods, but one god who can be understood only in three aspects. In the words of the hymn "Holy, Holy, Holy," written by the English Bishop of Calcutta, Reginald Heber (1783–1826), the Christian deity is "God in one person, blessed Trinity."

Superficially at least, Zoroastrianism—the main religion of Persia (modern Iran) from the sixth century BCE to the seventh century CE—appears not to be monotheistic. It features two main gods—Ahura Mazda, the principle of goodness, and Ahriman (or Angra Mainyu), the principle of darkness. Since Ahura Mazda defeats Ahriman, however, this religion, too, is ultimately monotheistic.

Hinduism, Sikhism, and Buddhism

The major religions of southern and eastern Asia also have monotheistic aspects, but they are not exclusive in the same way as Judaism, Christianity, and Islam. Hindu monotheism requires loving devotion to Vishnu or Siva, the supreme god who will reward his followers by saving them from the cycle of rebirths to which they will otherwise be subjected for eternity, but it also permits the existence of lesser divinities—in all, there are six million of them. This may resemble polytheism, but it is different because Hinduism is founded on the belief that every thing but one is an illusion (*maya*). The only thing that really exists is known as The One, or Ultimate Reality. All divinities and human souls share in The One, which is conceived of personally as the creator god, Brahma, or impersonally as Brahman, an abstract that emphasizes unity. According to the *Upanishads*, Sanskrit sacred books composed between 400 and 200 BCE, Brahman may join with atman, the individual soul, in a mystical act of union known as yoga. When any one god is worshiped, he or she takes on the powers of all the others.

The Sikh religion is an outgrowth of Hinduism and Islam. It was founded by Guru Nanak (1469–1539), a mystic whose core values were Hindu but who was also deeply influenced by Muslim teachings. He believed in a monotheistic deity, whom he designated Sat Nam ("true name"), who had created all men equal. This emphasis on equality inspired Guru Nanak to denounce the Hindu caste system, which viewed workers as inferior citizens, and insist upon the dignity of labor. He reacted against

Left: The 14th-century-BCE pharaoh Amenhotep IV—shown here on a contemporary bas-relief—tried unsuccessfully to establish monotheism in Egypt. He instituted the sole worship of the sun god Aton, depicted as the sun disk in the top right of the image.

Banished from the Pantheon

Muhammad (c. 570–632 CE), the prophet of Islam, ousted all but one of the deities that had formerly been worshiped in Arabia. Although Allah was destined to become the one true Muslim god, he had previously been just one of many occupants of the Arabian pantheon. Among the others were Allat, the Syrian moon goddess; al-Manat, goddess of fate; and al-Uzza, a fertility goddess associated with the planet Venus. Al-Uzza was the chosen deity of Muhammad's own tribe, but even she was banished as monotheism took over.

Right: This bas-relief from the second century CE from a temple in Palmyra, Syria, depicts Allat, one of the deities displaced by Islam.

ritual as practiced by both Hindus and Muslims, and attached paramount importance to the conduct of the individual. That belief is reflected in the most strikingly original aspect of Sikhism, namely the way in which it recognizes one supreme being but leaves individual Sikhs to decide whether to interpret the doctrine monotheistically (one god only), pantheistically (god and the world are one), or monistically (all things, divine and mortal, form a single unity).

Buddhism, which emerged in the fifth century BCE and was also a development of Hinduism, is strictly not a theistic religion at all—in other words, it has no god. Originally its practitioners simply followed the teachings of Gautama Buddha, a prince who had attained nirvana, or enlightenment, and through it escaped the endless cycle of reincarnation. Gradually, however, Buddhists in Southeast Asia came to regard Gautama as if he were the supreme deity. Similarly, many Japanese people worship Amida Buddha as the one savior God. Buddhist meditation aims to bring the meditator into a state of oneness with all being, in which state his or her individuality disappears.

Africa and North America

Most European scholars of the 19th century took the view that religions evolved from nature worship through pantheism to monotheism, which they regarded as the best, most highly developed, and "right" theology. Subsequent research, however, has revealed that numerous civilizations in Africa and North America moved in exactly the opposite direction. Many people on both continents believe in a supreme deity or High God who has simply left the earth to its own devices. Ritual acts of worship and the creation of images of the deity are therefore pointless. After the High God went away,

polytheistic practices emerged in honor of local natural forces, ancestors, and animals.

In the opinion of some observers, however, the ultimate aim of such rituals is to reunite worshipers with the supreme being, whoever or wherever he or she may be. Thus it may be argued that these religions are monotheistic, even though the one god has not been identified or located.

Meanwhile, several Native American peoples have adopted a single object of worship. One such deity is Wakan Tanka, the Great Spirit, or creator god, of the Sioux. Attempts to pigeonhole this god as a monotheistic deity, however, are undermined by the fact that he is attended by other, lesser powers, in much the same way as the Christian God is served by angels and saints who are "venerated," rather than "worshiped." In practice, the line between veneration and worship is often indistinctly drawn.

Left: An Apsaroke, photographed c. 1908, attaches himself to a pole with thongs as part of the Sun Dance. The pole itself symbolizes the central source of spiritual power. The Native American belief in a central power—often known as a Great Spirit—has a monotheistic aspect, although the spirit is often attended by lesser beings.

Although monotheism is clearly defined as belief in one god, it is clear that, in practice, few monotheistic religions are as pure and simple as that. Even Judaism has Shekinah (Hebrew: "presence of god"), a manifestation of the divine presence that is similar to the Holy Spirit of Christianity. Neither is Islam purely monotheistic in the dictionary sense of the term. It honors Muhammad, Abraham, and Jesus Christ as prophets, and assigns them semidivine powers.

For monotheists who draw on the Old Testament, the god in which they believe is the one true god. His essence and character are taken to be unique and entirely different from those of all other beings that might be considered comparable, especially the equivalent gods of other religions. God in monotheism is the creator of the world and everyone and everything in it. Unlike his theistic equivalents, he does not abandon his creation but leads it using his infinite power and wisdom—he is omnipotent, omniscient, and everlasting. Consequently, everything that has ever happened or will happen is a manifestation of divine will. Since, unlike the gods of pantheism, he is also a personal god, it may reasonably be said that everything is in his hands. Yet despite the fact that he is imagined as human in form, he is holy and infinitely mysterious—mortal humans love him and fear him because of his power, but also fear him because of their inability to understand him fully.

Attitudes to other beliefs

Historically, another significant characteristic of monotheism has been its attitude to other faiths. It rejects all other belief systems as false religions, often denouncing them as "idolatrous." This rejection partly explains the aggression that has often been displayed by adherents of monotheistic religions toward other faiths. Over time, this intolerance has hardened: while the Old Testament of the Bible merely described the gods of other religions as impostors or demons, later adherents of Judaism, Christianity, and also of Islam took the more extreme view that their god was the only god, and that the others did not exist at all. The consequences of exclusive monotheism continue to have major repercussions to this day.

BARBARA GARDNER

Bibliography
Armstrong, Karen. *A History of God.* New York: Knopf, 1993.
Dietrich, Wendell S. *Ethical Monotheistic Religion and Theory of Culture.* Atlanta, GA: Scholars Press, 1986.
Goodman, Lenn. *Monotheism.* Totowa, NJ: Allanheld, Osmun, 1981.
Kirsch, Jonathan. *God Against the Gods: The History of the War Between Polytheism and Monotheism.* New York: Viking Press, 2004.

SEE ALSO: Africa; Animism; Arabia; Great Spirit; India; Iran; Native Americans; Nature Religions; Paganism; Polytheism; Prehistoric Religion.

MOON

Ancient worship of the moon varied around the world. Some cultures viewed the moon as a benevolent entity; others saw it as an evil, fearsome deity of the night. Most, however, looked to the phases of the moon for more practical purposes, seeing them as a means of deciding when to plant or harvest crops, or as a way to predict the change of seasons.

In most world mythologies the moon is thought of in relation to the sun, and a common motif is that the moon and the sun are either siblings, spouses, or both. Sometimes they represent a primordial couple that creates life. In some cases the two are lovers, tragically doomed to be parted except during eclipses. More often, however, their relationship is hostile, even murderous, because neither wants to share the sky with the other. Coyolxauhqui, the warrior moon goddess of the Aztecs, for example, was hounded every morning by her half brother, the sun, who eventually decapitated her. Coyolxauhqui's severed head was thrown up to the sky, where it became the moon.

Another story of sibling enmity between the sun and the moon is found in Inuit mythology. Hidden in darkness, a brother violated a powerful taboo and seduced his sister. Curious, she secretly marked her lover's face with soot before his departure. When she later discovered his identity, she was so horrified that she sliced off one of the breasts he had so passionately caressed in the night. Making a torch of it, she escaped into the heavens, where she became

Above: Ancient peoples were fascinated by the moon and explained its creation in various stories: often the moon was thought of as female.

Siqiniq, the sun goddess. Her brother lit another torch and pursued her until his torch flickered out. He became Taqqiq, the moon.

Africa, too, has myths depicting hostility between the sun and the moon. Often such myths—like others around the world—offer explanations for the phases of the moon. For example, the San believe that every 30 or so days the moon, a male, angers the sun, also male. In revenge the sun turns his rays into sharp knives and begins slicing up the moon, which represents the waning phases of the moon

leading to the new moon. When almost nothing of the moon is left, he pleads for his life. The sun, no longer finding any satisfaction in abusing the moon, withdraws and lets the moon recover. The moon grows to full size—in other words, passing through the waxing phases leading to the full moon—at which time the sun's anger flares anew and he resumes slicing up the moon once again.

The moon in Egypt

In ancient Egypt the moon could be either a male or a female deity. The god of the underworld, Osiris, also represented the regular phases of the moon. In one famous legend Seth, a rival god, kills Osiris and cuts his body to pieces. The dismembered body of Osiris may have represented the nights of the waning moon; the pieces of the corpse were then reassembled and given life by his wife, Isis.

A more general moon god was Khonsu, the son of Amun and Mut, the patron god and goddess of Thebes. Khonsu was depicted either with a falcon's head or as a baboon. He was originally connected with childbirth and later gained fame for his ability to drive out evil spirits.

Egypt's most famous lunar deity, however, was Thoth, associated with the left eye, or moon eye, of the sun god, Re. Like many moon deities, this ibis-headed god had strong links to magic, healing, language, writing, and record keeping. In addition to his ibis form, he was also depicted, like Khonsu, as a squatting baboon ecstatically welcoming the dawn. His cult was centered at the city of Hermopolis (today the village of Al-Ashmounein on the Nile), where he took over the functions of older deities.

Preceding Thoth at Hermopolis was a much more ancient moon goddess, the frog-headed Heqet. Among Heqet's titles were primordial mother of all existence, goddess of birth, and midwife goddess. In addition to her lunar role she was associated with transformation, sorcery, magic, the final stages of birth, and the underworld.

Other Egyptian deities associated with the moon were Isis; the cat goddess Bastet; Thoth's wife Seshat; the cobra goddess Wadjet; and the goddess of music and dance, Hathor. Hathor, who wore the sun disk above her head, was usually associated with the sun, but she also represented the festive, social aspect of the moon. Wadjet was the sun's womb and tomb, yet she did her work in the papyrus swamps of the night, where, according to some texts, the moon was her eye.

Left: This sculpture of Thoth, dated about 600 BCE, shows the god with the head of an ibis.

Indian journey of the dead

According to the *Upanishads*—writings from the pre-Hindu Vedic beliefs of ancient India—the moon is where the dead go to await rebirth. During the first half of their stay, their breathing spirits nurture their host, Chandra, the moon god. During the second half of their stay, a replenished Chandra shapes their next incarnation.

Hindus believe that the god Soma represents the moon. Like the Greek goddess Selene, Soma, as the moon, rides a chariot across the night sky. Soma was also the name of a powerful drink meant only for the gods, granting them immortality. Because the drink was intoxicating, the god Soma was also associated with drunkenness.

Different personalities of the moon

While some cultures have viewed the moon as a benevolent entity, others have seen it as evil. Among the Bantu speakers of Africa, for example, the Luba people regard the male moon as a royal hero because he brings fertility and rain; they view his brother-in-law, the sun, as their enemy, for he dries up the moon's precious moisture. In contrast, the Lunda people, also Bantu speakers, regard the sun as their royal hero and the moon as an evil, sterile princess who brings the dry season.

Moon Deities from Around the World	
Aztec:	Coyolxauhqui
Babylonian:	Sin
Baltic:	Menesis
Chinese:	Shing-Moo
Egyptian:	Heqet, Khonsu, Thoth, and others
Fon (Benin):	Mawu
Greek:	Artemis, Hecate, Selene
Indian (Vedic):	Chandra
Inuit:	Taqqiq
Irish (Celtic):	Brigit, Danu
Japanese (Shinto):	Tsuki-yomi
Maya:	Ix Chel
Phrygian:	Cybele
Roman:	Diana, Luna
Sumerian:	Innana, Lilith

Below: The magnificent frescoes in the temple at Tulúm in the Yucatán Peninsula make it one of the most visited Maya sites in Mexico. Dedicated to the moon, the buildings were constructed around 1200 CE, when the civilization was rapidly declining.

Goddesses and Lunatics

In ancient Greece three female deities were associated with the moon: Artemis, Hecate, and Selene. Artemis, who was adopted by the Romans as Diana, was also the virgin goddess of the wilderness and the hunt. Hecate was, according to some sources, the daughter of Demeter, goddess of grain and harvest. Hecate's sister was the more famous Persephone, queen of the underworld, who was allowed to spend part of the year on Mount Olympus with Demeter, during which time the crops grew.

Of the three goddesses it was Selene, whose name means "moon," who was most closely identified with the moon in ancient Greece. She was the sister of Helios, the sun god. Like her brother, she rode in a chariot, but hers lit up the night sky in a modest way compared to Helios's more luminous chariot, which gave the earth daylight.

In Rome Selene became known as Luna, the Latin word for *moon*, and it is from the name *Luna* that words such as *lunar* and *lunacy* have evolved. The word *lunacy* is linked to the moon because it used to be thought that insanity (lunacy) was caused by phases of the moon. As recently as the late 19th century, insane asylums in many parts of the world regularly called in extra staff to work on nights of a full moon. Recent misconceptions about effects of the moon include the notion that emergency calls to police or fire services are more common when there is a full moon.

Among the Baltic peoples of northern Europe the sun goddess was Saule, who watched over mortals in general, women in childbirth, and orphans in particular. She also welcomed the dead into her celestial apple tree. Her partner was the moon god, Menulis and together they had many children that were the stars. However, Menulis became very lazy, and did not rise in the mornings. One day Saule found their daughter, a star named Little Sun, or Saules Meita, by a river looking very unhappy. It emerged that Menulis had raped her. Saule was so furious at the injury done to her daughter that she slashed her husband's face, making certain that the scars were deep enough to last forever. Then she banished him to the night.

Below: The full moon is widely supposed to inspire outlandish or even evil behavior, but there is no scientific evidence to support the concept of lunacy.

A Chilean people, the Araucanians, have an even darker view than the Balts, for they regard the sun and all deities as malignant—all except for the female moon, who protects them from the others and changes the color of her skin to enable her people to foretell the future.

The Mayan moon goddess

Another story in which the the sun's relationship with the moon is hostile is the tragic tale of Ix Chel. She was a moon goddess and a goddess of fertility, and medicine, who was worshiped for some 900 years by the Maya—a Native American people who lived in the region from southern Mexico to El Salvador. Like many lunar goddesses, she was a weaver artist. She wove alone and traveled through the night skies with her loom sticks crossed in front of her, protecting herself and her artistry from wild jaguars hiding among the stars. Ix Chel felt so fully complete in herself and her work that she had no genitals and had no desire to give birth.

When Ix Chel and the sun married, he forced her to submit to him. Since he desired to have sexual intercourse with her, the sun had a deer trample Ix Chel in order to create a vagina in her. In another version of the myth, the sun tore out one of Ix Chel's eyes to prevent her from shining so brightly.

The creation of the moon

Many scientists believe that when our solar system was young, the moon was originally part of Earth. After a collision with an object the size of the planet Mars, the moon broke away, forming its own orbit around Earth. From then on the moon has provided reflected secondary light from the sun, partially illuminating the night.

Without the moon, there would have been no safe niche in which life as we know it could ever have evolved. There would be no stable weather patterns, no seasons, and no way to gauge when to plant and harvest food. The moon's gravitational field enabled Earth's axis to stablilize. Without it, Earth's relatively steady axis would wobble erratically, so that a region that was frozen one year could become a barren inferno a few years later. People would have to construct homes that could withstand such radical and ever-changing climatic extremes. Polar caps would freeze and melt ceaselessly, making coastal life impossible. Earth would slow its rotation to 20-hour days, losing at least four hours of darkness, which would increase the planet's exposure to the sun and send daytime temperatures soaring.

Other moon creation theories include one in which originally the moon formed away from Earth and Earth's gravitational field captured it, and put it in orbit.

Lycanthropy and Werewolves

The psychological condition in which a person believes that he or she is transformed into a wolf, or some other dangerous animal, is known as lycanthropy. The word comes from Greek roots, *lykos* (wolf) and *anthropos* (man). Lycanthropy occurs in many parts of the world, including Europe, northern Asia, Africa, and India.

In folklore a person who changes into a wolf is called a werewolf. In the most famous werewolf legends the person is transformed involuntarily during a full moon, although werewolf legends are not always associated with phases of the moon. Generally, it was believed that there were two ways for a person to become a werewolf. He or she either inherited the curse or was turned into a werewolf if bitten by another werewolf. Each month with the appearance of the full moon, the cursed person would transform completely—physically and mentally—into a large wolf to savage people and other animals, only returning to human form with the arrival of dawn.

In Europe, werewolf lore was common from the Balkans to France. In 16th-century France the fear of werewolves was so strong that many people who were believed to be real werewolves were burned werewolves.

Above: This German woodcut from the 16th century CE depicts a traveler under attack from a wolf that shape-shifted from a man.

The Moon in Prehistory

It is thought that humans began marking the regular changes of the seasons and phases of the moon long before the invention of accurate calendars. The earliest-known example seems to be the 13 lines carved on a crescent-moon-shaped horn held by the Venus of Laussel, a prehistoric cave sculpture in the Dordogne in France. The sculpture is thought to be more than 20,000 years old. Many historians argue that the markings represent a lunar year of 13 months, but others suggest that they might also represent the nights during which the moon is waxing.

Irish megalithic stones have many carvings of winding serpents whose wavy lines seem to symbolize lunar time—it has been suggested that the snake's ability to shed its skin and reemerge alive makes it among the oldest of lunar symbols. Many of the undulating serpents have 14-to-17 turnings, which represent the nights of lunar waxing plus the three-night period of the full moon. The longest serpents have 30 turnings, representing approximately the 29.5 days in a lunar month.

Historians have also pointed out that similar wavy-line patterns, most in the 14 to 17 range of turnings, have been found carved into antler bone from the Mesolithic period (c. 10,000–c. 8000 BCE) in northern Europe and in ceramics from east-central Europe from 6000 BCE. A similar kind of time-reckoning using wavy lines appears to date from Europe's Upper Paleolithic period (c. 27,000–19,000 BCE). Because many of these objects were connected with burials, the use of coiling snakes to represent the waxing life force points to a widespread belief that the dead, like the moon serpents, would themselves be regenerated.

Left: This Paleolithic sculpture, discovered on the wall of a cave in the Dordogne region of France, shows a woman now known as the Venus of Laussel. The exact purpose of the horn in her hand is unknown, but it is thought to be a calendar.

The effects of the moon's cycles

The moon's own gravitational pull has an influence on ocean tides and other cyclical phenomena. A common phenomenon that occurs among women when they live or spend a large amount of time together is the synchronization of their monthly menstrual cycles. In some communal-based African cultures this phenomenon gave women, in the eyes of their men, an enviable, even frightening, rapport with the moon and its phases.

The moon's regular phases also gave early civilizations a dependable reference point on which to base their calendars. Since the moon and the bodies of women were attuned to the same clock, ancient peoples had a reliable basis for measuring time. In the English language, the nouns *moon*, *menses* (menstrual flow), and *month* all share a common linguistic root that is connected with measurement. A month was one lunar cycle—13 moon cycles marked the lunar year.

In prehistoric times measuring such cycles gave crucial information to people about timing their migrations and hunts, and storing sufficient food for the winter. Later, when agriculture became more important than hunting, lunar cycles continued to play a crucial role. The moon's phases marked planting times. Today many people still believe that sowing seed either at or just before the new moon leads to significantly increased crops; others favor planting at the full moon.

Studies carried out in Germany in the 1920s and 1930s found that sowing seeds two days before the full moon did indeed seem to result in unusually rapid germination and subsequent robust health of crops. The germination and growth of seeds sown only two days later were delayed by eight days and never caught up to pre-full-moon plants. Researchers were unable to come up with a convincing explanation of the results, however, or of the role of the moon. Although much folklore says that root vegetables, such as carrots, should be planted only when the moon is dark, and above-ground plants only during the waxing moon, the German studies found that this was not true: both types of plants did better when planted 48 hours before the full moon.

The moon also marks the time of harvest. Just as with planting, some cultures believed it was better to harvest during the waxing phases, while others believed the waning phases were more beneficial.

The moon in weather lore

Long before scientists understood that the moon's gravitational field was essential for the stability of Earth's weather patterns, weather folklore paid careful respect to the moon. Interpretations of moon halos and "horns" (the crescent moon's pointed ends) are among the most ancient forms of predicting the weather. In Russia, for example, sharp, clear horns in spring indicated that a hot summer was on its way. As winter drew closer, those same sharp horns meant that mild weather would follow; if the horns looked fuzzy or blunted, frost was on its way. People in rural England believed that water in irrigated fields would not freeze until the moon rose: the reflected moonlight would then form the germ around which ice needles formed.

According to various cultures, a steady halo around the moon usually indicated that the weather would change for the worse. In Russia, for instance, it could simply mean the wind would rise. A red ring appearing only briefly meant that good weather was on its way. Two such red rings, however, or a single pale one, indicated frost or, if the rings were broken, snow.

Fact-based superstitions

Folk beliefs about the moon's effect on the weather are often dismissed as superstitions, yet there may be an underlying scientific basis for at least some of the folklore. Regarding the full moon's connection to frosts, for

Below: Every year at the time of the full harvest moon, people in Brittany, France, perform a ritual known as Return of the Gleaners. Gleaners are people who collect edible leftovers after the main crop has been gathered in.

Above: Ancient peoples had many stories to explain the striking "horned" appearance of the crescent moon. They also learned to interpret the clarity of the horns to predict weather conditions.

Moon Halos and Their Meaning

Moon halos could indicate events other than meteorological ones. An 18th-century Russian manuscript, which was probably based on much older sources, interprets the appearance of moon halos in all the months except February:

March:	Great czars and princes will do battle from east to west.
April:	There will be much fruit.
May:	Great hailstorms will occur.
June:	There will be war.
July:	There will be death to animals.
August:	Fish and honey will be plentiful.
September:	There will be little rain.
October:	The summer will be dry.
November:	There will be war.
December:	There will be famine.
January:	There will be great rains.

example, studies in the United States, Canada, north Wales, South Africa, India, and Australia have revealed that there is a regular drop in temperature for several days around the time of the full moon. These falls in temperature occur regardless of latitude or sea level. Likewise, American studies in 1962 indicated a strong connection between the moon and rainfall: researchers found that lunar phases could account for nearly 65 percent of rainfall changes in the United States. Australian studies produced similar results.

The exact role of the moon has been much speculated on since prehistory. Although many of the theories about its influence have been fanciful, there is no doubt that Earth's one natural satellite does have a major impact on the planet, even if the exact nature of this influence is still not clear.

KATHLEEN JENKS

Bibliography
Cashford, Jules. *The Moon: Myth and Image*. New York: Four Walls Eight Windows, 2003.
Mackenzie, Dana. *The Big Splat, or How Our Moon Came to Be*. New York: John Wiley and Sons, 2003.

SEE ALSO: Africa; Artemis; Aztecs; Baltic, The; Calendars; Creation Myths; Egypt; Festivals; India; Lycaon; Maya; Natural Forces; Selene; Sun.

MORPHEUS

In Greek and Roman mythology, Morpheus was originally the guardian of dreams. A son of Hypnos (Sleep) and Pasithea, the oldest of the Graces, he was generally depicted as a rotund, sleeping child with wings. It was only much later that poets began to identify him as the god of sleep.

The name *Morpheus* is derived from the Greek word *morphe*, meaning "shape." Morpheus and his brothers were said to have been the originators of the shapes and figures that appear in dreams. Morpheus could take on the form and behavior of any human; one of his brothers, Phobetor, could assume that of

any other creature; and another, Phantasos, that of any object. They lived in dark, cavernous places near the entrance to the underworld, the land of their uncle Thanatos (Death), the brother of Hypnos.

The earliest existing reference to Morpheus occurs in *Metamorphoses* by Ovid (43 BCE–17 CE). The poet tells the story of how Ceyx and Halcyone, the king and queen of Trachis (an ancient city in Thessaly, central Greece), were so happy that they referred to themselves as Zeus and Hera, the supreme king and queen of the gods. For this act of pride they were punished terribly. Ceyx was washed away in a storm at sea, and Hera ordered Hypnos to convey the bad news to Halcyone. The god of sleep sent his son, Morpheus, into the queen's dreams, where he assumed the

Below: Halcyone Discovering Ceyx, *a marble carving by English sculptor Thomas Banks (1735–1805). In Greek legend, Morpheus tells Halcyone of Ceyx's death by appearing to her in a dream in the form of her drowned husband.*

needed to set out on his final journey home. By contrast, in the same author's *Iliad*, Zeus sends a deceptive dream to Agamemnon, leader of the Greek army besieging Troy, to mislead him into taking the wrong course of action.

Dreams also featured prominently in certain ancient Greek religious practices. There were numerous oracles whose responses to questions were transmitted through dreams, and at many healing centers patients seeking cures slept out in the holiest areas of the sanctuaries in the hope of dreaming about their treatment and recovery.

Interpreting dreams has been practiced for millennia. Ancient Egyptians and Babylonians, who recorded dreams and their interpretations, believed dreaming was a method of communication with the gods; prophetic dreams are alluded to in many west Asian texts, notably the Bible. Most ancient Greeks believed that dreams served a predictive function, but Greek philosopher Aristotle (384–322 BCE) perceived dreams to be more expressive of the dreamer's senses and emotions than future events.

form of the drowned Ceyx and announced his own death. Halcyone, overcome with grief, committed suicide by jumping off a cliff into the sea. Finally the gods took pity and turned Ceyx and Halcyone into kingfishers, or halcyons, and calmed the winds during their breeding season. This is the origin of the phrase *halcyon days,* meaning a period of peace and tranquillity.

The memory of dreams

Although Morpheus himself does not appear until the work of Ovid, the idea that dreams contained important messages from the gods was a common feature in Greek literature from centuries earlier. There, deities might appear in the form of individual humans in order to warn, threaten, or impart information to the dreamer. The information thus conveyed may have been literally true or it may have been cryptically deceptive. Either way, the mind of the dreamer was being infiltrated by a god who meant to influence the course of events in the world of mortals. Thus in the *Odyssey* by Homer, Greek epic poet of the ninth or eighth century BCE, the goddess Athena appears to Phaeacian princess Nausicaa in a dream in the guise of one of Nausicaa's friends. Athena's intention was to stir the princess to action so that she would meet the shipwrecked Odysseus in an apparently chance encounter and give him the help he

Morpheus in art

Morpheus rarely appeared in the art of antiquity and the Middle Ages. However, the god became more prominent in western Europe after the Renaissance. He is alluded to in the poem "Il Penseroso" by English author John Milton (1608–1674) and in various songs by English composers Henry Purcell (c. 1659–1695) and Georg Friedrich Handel (1685–1759). Morpheus became even more popular with the Romantic movement of the 19th century, and his name was often invoked as a figure representing the whole world of sleep and unconsciousness as well as dreams. Association of the name Morpheus with an entity that exercises powerful control over the human mind, especially in a narcotic state, led Friedrich W. A. Sertürner (1783–1841), the German pharmacist who first extracted the juice of the poppy seed in 1805, to name his pain-relieving product "morphine."

ANTHONY BULLOCH

Bibliography

Homer, and Robert Fagles, trans. *The Iliad and the Odyssey.* New York: Penguin Books, 1999.

Ovid, and A. D. Melville, trans. *Metamorphoses.* New York: Oxford University Press, 1998.

SEE ALSO: Agamemnon; Athena; Hypnos; Odysseus; Zeus.

MUSES

In Greek and Roman mythology, the Muses were the nine goddesses of all artistic, intellectual, and scientific pursuits. They were the daughters of Zeus (Jupiter) and Mnemosyne, goddess of memory. Their names were Calliope, Clio, Erato, Euterpe, Melpomene, Polymnia, Terpsichore, Thalia, and Urania.

The nine Muses had separate identities and special areas of responsibility. Each was commonly depicted with something evocative of her particular expertise. Calliope was in charge of epic and heroic poetry; she held a writing tablet and a stylus. Clio, the Muse of history, clasped a half-opened roll of parchment. Erato inspired lyric and erotic poetry; she played a small lyre. Euterpe was responsible for music, especially wind instruments, or lyric poetry; she played a double flute. Melpomene, the Muse of tragic poetry, held a tragic mask. Polymnia looked after sacred poetry, hymns, and mime; she was normally portrayed looking modest and pensive, with one finger raised to her lips. Terpsichore was the goddess of dance and choral poetry and song; she was usually seen dancing and holding a large lyre. Thalia, the Muse of comedy and bucolic, or rustic, poetry, held a comic mask and carried a shepherd's crook. Urania was the Muse of astronomy; she pointed at or held a globe and sometimes also carried scientific instruments.

Overlapping roles

The ancients, however, did not adhere tightly to this neat arrangement of one job for each goddess—they usually invoked the Muse of their choice, regardless of her traditional role. For example, Homer, a Greek epic poet of the ninth or eighth century BCE, described the Muses as

Below: This painting, entitled Dance of Apollo and the Muses, *is by Italian artist Baldassare Peruzzi (1481–1536).*

singers in a choir performing at a banquet of the gods; in this he was followed by many later writers. Roman poet Horace (65–8 BCE) called on Melpomene rather than Erato to help him write his "Aeolian" (lyric) verse.

Springs of inspiration

From time to time the Muses inhabited numerous locations, but one of their perennial favorite haunts was Mount Helicon, a large mountain in Boeotia (a region in central Greece). It was there that Greek poet Hesiod

Below: This mosaic from the third century CE depicts Virgil, flanked by the Muses Clio and Melpomene, writing the Aeneid.

(fl. 800 BCE) claimed to have been inspired by drinking the waters of the Hippocrene, a sacred spring that was said to have been created by the winged horse Pegasus with a kick of his hooves.

According to legend, the Muses danced around the Hippocrene, singing songs about the Olympian gods, the adventures of heroes, and the creation of the world. Mortal artists, musicians, and poets could not hope to tackle these or any other subjects without first beseeching the Muses to imbue them with their divine power. "Tell me, Muse, of the man of many turns," prayed Homer as he began his epic poem the *Odyssey*. "Help me, O Muse, to recall the reasons why," asked Virgil (70–19 BCE) at the start of the *Aeneid*.

The Muses were often at pains to stress the distinction between what they had to offer—inspiration—and what humans may, in their limited way, have been looking for in art—the truth. The nine goddesses answered the prayers of Hesiod thus: "Listen, you country bumpkins, you swag-bellied yahoos, we know how to tell many lies that pass for truth, and we know, when we wish, how to tell the truth itself." Yet although they are not always strictly truthful, the Muses playfully tease out an artistic truth that may be deeper than mere fact. They are, after all, trying to communicate with humans, who can never fully comprehend the workings of the gods. Therefore they must impart to mortals knowledge that has been manipulated and elevated by art. Thus it is only after the nine sisters have plucked a branch from a laurel tree in full bloom and given it to Hesiod for a staff, while breathing into him their divine song, that he can find the appropriate words to describe the birth of the deathless gods. "Happy the one whom the Muses love," says the "Homeric Hymn to the Muses," "for from his lips the speech flows sweetly."

Another spring, the Aganippe, in an area known as the Vale of the Muses at the foot of Mount Helicon near Thespiae, was also sacred to the nine deities. It was there that the Thespians—the local people whose name has since become a synonym for *actors*—honored the goddesses every five years with a series of competitions in a wide range of disciplines, including poetry composition, playing the Kithara (a lyrelike musical instrument), and devising tragedy and comedy. Excavations in the Vale of the Muses have uncovered the theater in which these contests were held, a temple with an attached stoa (a covered walkway with a colonnade) for votive offerings, and the bases of nine statues inscribed with epigrams of the poet Onestos. Roman poet Catullus (c. 84–c. 54 BCE) summoned the Muses to come from Aganippe to lend their song to the wedding of a certain Junia Aurunculeia. In the *Eclogues*, Virgil complained of their absence from Aganippe while Gallus pined away for his beloved Lycoris nearby.

Pierian springs

Among the water sources that were sacred to the Muses were the Pierian springs in the foothills of Mount Olympus in Thrace, part of what later became Macedonia. This was the native land of Orpheus, the mythical musician and poet who, according to some accounts, was a son of Calliope. A ceramic tile of the region dating from about 440 BCE depicts six Muses holding instruments and watching as Orpheus's severed head is retrieved from the water. The composition of the scene suggests that

Choosing between a God and a Satyr

In a well-known classical story, the Muses were called to judge a musical contest between the god Apollo and Marsyas, a satyr from Phrygia (part of modern Turkey). When the goddess Athena abandoned the double flute because playing it distorted her face, Marsyas took it up and became famous for his beautiful music. He challenged Apollo to a musical contest: the winner could do whatever he liked with the loser. At first the players matched each other, note for note, but Apollo then challenged Marsyas to play his instrument upside down. Apollo could do this without difficulty on his instrument, the lyre, but on the flute the task was impossible. The Muses therefore awarded the contest to Apollo, who suspended Marsyas from a pine tree and flayed him alive. The Marsyas River is said to have formed either from the blood of the satyr or from the tears of his friends. In another version of the story, the contest was judged by Midas, who declared Marsyas the winner; Apollo punished Midas by giving him the ears of an ass. Marsyas became a popular subject in Roman art, and a statue of him stood in the Forum in Rome.

Orpheus's head will continue to sing songs and give oracles under the inspiration of the Muses. Orpheus's student (or, according to some accounts, teacher) Musaeus, who was supposed to have spread the Orphic cult, obviously takes his name from the goddesses.

According to Roman poet Ovid (43 BCE–17 CE), the nine daughters of king Pierus of Pella impiously assumed the names of the Muses and challenged the supremacy of the genuine Helicon goddesses. They even dared to wager that their own Pierian springs were a greater source of inspiration than those of the Hippocrene and Aganippe. The Helicon Muses soundly defeated the princesses in a song contest, and then turned the mortal upstarts into magpies. In other accounts, notably that of Diodorus Siculus (90–21 BCE), Archelaus, king of Macedonia in the fifth century BCE, organized dramatic and athletic festivals at Dion (near Mount Olympus) lasting nine days, one day for each of the Muses. King Philip II of Macedonia (382–336 BCE) used to make grand sacrifices at Dion to Zeus and the nine Muses to celebrate his military victories, and his son Alexander the Great (356–323 BCE) feasted there in their honor before setting off on his conquest of Asia. In the same way, Spartans traditionally sacrificed to the Muses before doing battle; they marched forth from their city not to the sound of trumpets, but to flute and lyre accompaniment.

Below: This statue of Polymnia, muse of divine poetry, is housed in the Vatican Museum, Rome, Italy.

The Music of the Spheres

In the minds of historians there is no doubt that the ancient Greeks comprehended the workings of the universe in terms of musical harmonies. We still speak of the "music of the spheres," for example, a notion that is derived from the Pythagoreans and Plato. This belief in the musicality of the universe is reflected in the Muses themselves. They were born from the supreme god Zeus, or perhaps even from the Titan Uranus, and serve as the only source of information humans have about the heavens. The Pythagoreans in fact made the Muses special patrons of their schools and gave special primacy to the cult of the nine goddesses. Memory is the basis of artistic performance, which the Muses personified, and it figures in Pythagorean doctrines about the transmigration of souls. The idea is that the soul retains a memory, put there by the Muses, of its former lives (or for Plato, of the ideal forms with which it came in contact in a prenatal state). The recollection of our past lives helps us eventually to escape the cycle of life and achieve immortal immutability, the blessed state of the gods.

Greek geographer and historian Pausanias (143–176 CE) gave a different version of the legend. According to him, the cult of the Muses had been established by Ephialtes and Otus, sons of Poseidon, at Ascra, the town they had founded at the foot of Mount Helicon. These brothers believed that the Muses were three in number—Melete (Meditation or Practice), Mneme (Memory), and Aoede (Song). When Pierus came to Thespiae he discovered that there were actually nine Muses, and it was he who gave them the names that have come down to us. Pausanias suggests that Pierus, a Macedonian, may have taken the number from the Thracians, who practiced a very old cult of the three Muses, but he also notes the tradition that Pierus himself had nine daughters. Pausanias cites a poem by Mimnermus (c. 630 BCE) that makes a distinction between the three Muses, who were daughters of Uranus, and the younger nine Muses, who were daughters of Zeus.

Other sources of inspiration

Yet another water source that was sacred to the Muses was the Castalian spring on the slopes of Mount Parnassus. There the Pythian Sibyl used to bathe before giving her oracular pronouncements. Likewise those who consulted the oracle had to cleanse themselves in the sacred spring and carry out other rites in order to obtain a response. This spring was close to Delphi, where the Muses came into contact with the god Apollo, who shared their interest in music. In the work of Pindar (c. 522–c. 438 BCE), the god is known as Apollo *Mousagetes* (leader of the Muses) because he strums the lyre while the "violet-tressed" goddesses sing and play along.

A new job for Heracles

Later, in Rome, this *Mousagetes* role was taken by Heracles. Although images of Heracles playing the lyre were not unknown in Greece, the traditional story was that the hero had struggled to learn music under the tutorship of Linus, a child of Urania, and that he had killed his teacher in a fit of rage and frustration. Nevertheless, after a successful campaign against Ambracia (later known as Árta, a city in western Greece) about 187 BCE, Roman general Marcus Fulvius Nobilior erected a temple in Rome in which he placed an image of Heracles playing the lyre along with images of the nine Muses. In the same year he placed a small and very old shrine to the Muses in the temple. Because of this the temple became known as Herculis Musarum Aedes (the Temple of Heracles of the Muses), which also may have led to Heracles being referred to as *Mousagetes*. Although the original temple may have been intended for the worship of the Muses themselves, the

statues within it suggest that there may have developed a cult of Hercules Musarum. This may have been invented by Quintus Pomponius Musa, a moneyer (a manufacturer of coins or a banker). The cult's festival was held annually on June 30 (Julian calendar), but nothing is known of the rituals that were performed on that day. The temple became a famous landmark: Roman statesman and author Cicero (106–43 BCE) described it as an outstanding example of how a man of war had turned to the arts of

Muses and Museums

In ancient Greece the *mouseion* or "museum" was an open space or a building devoted to collecting artwork inspired by the Muses. Ancient museums typically contained statues of the nine Muses, along with an altar or shrine. The first such museum was established at the foot of Mount Helicon in the Vale of the Muses. There, statues of mythical and historical musicians stood on display, along with archives of distinguished works of poetry. In ancient Alexandria, Egypt, the museum appears to have had other functions as well. In particular, it was used as a place for research, education, and literary discussion. Another smaller museum existed at Athens. As storehouses of Greek culture, museums did much to preserve literature and learning for later generations.

Below: Modern museums reflect their origins in collections of works inspired by the Muses.

peace. In the first century BCE, L. Marcius Philippus, the stepfather of Emperor Augustus, rebuilt and enhanced the temple with great splendor and increased its importance.

In Rome the Muses replaced the Camenae, an old set of Italic nymphs whose name they adopted. They inhabited a spring below the Caelian Hill, from where they inspired mortal songs, the best-known surviving examples of which are by Livius Andronicus (c. 284–c. 204 BCE) and Gnaeus Naevius (c. 270–c. 199 BCE). The Camenae continued to make occasional appearances in the work of later Roman writers, but usually only as a fanciful title for the Greek goddesses, while their festival on August 13 gradually faded into insignificance.

Blind with love

The Muses are associated with numerous characters of Greek myth who sing, play instruments, dance, or tell riddles. In one legend the mythical musician Thamyris, whom Linus taught to play the lyre, challenged the

goddesses to a contest. If he won, he would make love to all nine of them in succession; if he lost, they would take from him whatever they wished. The Muses won, naturally, and then deprived Thamyris of his eyesight and his musical skills. However, the loss of sight was not always a punishment from the Muses. According to Homer, the bard Demodocus was especially beloved by the Nine. As a mark of their affection, they blinded him, while at the same time blessing him with the gift of song and an unfailing memory (Homer himself may also have been blind).

Link with the Sphinx

When the Sirens challenged the supremacy of the Muses, they, too, were defeated and forced to submit to having their feathers plucked. The Muses also taught the nymph Echo her musical skills. After she had incurred the jealousy of Pan and been torn to shreds, they gave her dismembered parts the ability to make music all over the earth. The Sphinx that tormented Thebes is said to have learned her riddle from the Muses. According to Hesiod, when the Muses went to Mount Olympus to attend the banquets of the gods and provide the entertainment, they sat alongside the Graces (Charities), the goddesses of charm and attraction, and Himerous, the god of desire. Pausanias reported that at Troezen (an ancient Greek city on the northeast tip of the Peloponnese) there was an altar on which worshipers sacrificed to the Muses and to Hypnos, the god of sleep. The Muse Clio was often credited with the introduction of the alphabet into Greece, although in *Prometheus Bound*, a play by Aeschylus (525–456 BCE), the hero claims that he introduced it himself, and that the Muses took it up as one of their creative tools.

KIRK SUMMERS

Right:
This vase,
dating from the
fifth century BCE,
depicts Thamyris
being blinded by
the Muses.

Bibliography

Hesiod, and M. L. West, trans. *Theogony; and Works and Days*. New York: Oxford University Press, 1999.
Homer, and Robert Fagles, trans. *The Odyssey*. New York: Penguin USA, 1999.
Ovid, and A. D. Melville, trans. *Metamorphoses*. New York: Oxford University Press, 1998.

SEE ALSO: Apollo; Echo; Graces; Heracles; Mnemosyne; Orpheus; Sibyl; Sphinx; Titans; Uranus; Zeus.

Isis and *The Golden Ass*

The description of the mysteries of Isis by Roman writer Lucius Apuleius (c. 124–c. 170 CE) provides one of the most detailed descriptions of the secret at the heart of a mystery cult initiation. In *The Golden Ass* , the 1951 English translation of his work by poet Robert Graves (1895–1985), Apuleius says:

"I approached the very gates of death and set one foot on Proserpine's [Persephone's] threshold, yet was permitted to return, rapt through all the elements. At midnight I saw the sun shining as if it were noon; I entered the presence of the gods of the underworld and the gods of the upper-world, stood near and worshiped them."

The Isis Mysteries seem to have come closest in the ancient world to the idea of a universal great goddess who underlies all the individual goddesses of the various nations and peoples of the world. Apuleius addresses her as Ceres (Demeter), Venus (Aphrodite), Artemis, and Proserpine (Persephone), beseeching her help "by whatever name, in whatever aspect, with whatever ceremonies you deign to be invoked."

Isis, while claiming that name as her true one, notes that she is also Pessinuntica to the Phrygians, Cecropian Artemis to the Athenians, Paphian Aphrodite to the Cyprians, Dictynna to the Cretans, Stygian Proserpine to the Sicilians, Mother of the Corn to the Eleusinians, and Juno, Bellona, Hecate, and Rhamnubia to others.

Anthony and Cleopatra in 30 BCE. In the cosmopolitan cultures of Greece, Rome, Egypt, and parts of West Asia, people with different religious traditions lived side by side, largely harmoniously. There were many faiths to choose from, and a believer in any one of them would know that there were always people on the "inside" ("us") and people on the "outside" ("them"). Even during the Roman Empire (30 BCE–476 CE), as long as people participated in the state religion, it was acceptable for them also to take part in other religious practices and affiliations.

Almost anything could be regarded as having a mysterious aspect. Even the brotherhood that surrounded Greek thinker Pythagoras (c. 580–c. 500 BCE) was sometimes described as a mystery cult because its members discussed the possibility of a person's soul having life in another body after death. In fact, they were philosophers.

The most famous—and in many ways the most typical—mystery cult was the Greek Eleusinian Mysteries, so named because it was based at Eleusis, a seaside town on the outskirts of Athens. The essence of the Eleusinian Mysteries was the worship of Persephone, goddess of the underworld. She had been abducted to the underworld by Hades, the god of death. The lost girl was mourned so much by her mother, the grain goddess Demeter, that she was eventually allowed to divide her time between the two worlds. Henceforth Persephone spent the summer months on earth, and the winter in the underworld as Hades' queen.

The symbolism of this story is clear—Persephone represents the death of plants in fall and their rebirth in

Right: This painted statue of Isis was carved from limestone in Egypt in the third century CE.

spring. The initiation of new recruits seems to have begun with their immersion in the sea. They were then subjected to periods of darkness and light, and finally witnessed an ear of grain being cut and a priest enacting a kind of marriage ceremony that represented death and rebirth.

Mystery cults of Dionysus, Orpheus, and others

Among the other important Greek mysteries were those of Dionysus and Orpheus. The cult of Dionysus, the wine god, dates from no later than the second millennium BCE and was attended by enthusiastic female revelers (see box, page 932) known as Bacchants by the Romans, and maenads by the ancient Greeks. The exact nature of the rites is unclear, but the ceremonies seem to have featured music, dance, a trancelike state, and, of course, wine. When the Dionysia, as these seasonal festivals were called, were imported to Rome, they became the Bacchanalia (named for the Roman god Bacchus), a word that today has the meaning of debauched, alcoholic revelry.

The Villa of the Mysteries

In August 79 CE Mount Vesuvius in southern Italy erupted violently. Within 24 hours of the eruption the cities closest to the volcano, Herculaneum and Pompeii, were buried underneath 10 feet (3 m) of volcanic ash and debris. It all happened so fast that many inhabitants of the two cities were caught in the deluge of ash as they desperately tried to escape. Because the ash layer was airtight, many buildings and objects such as frescoes (wall paintings) in and around the two cities were preserved beneath it.

On a road between the two cities lies the Villa of the Mysteries, which was discovered in 1909. It was covered by ash from the eruption, preserving within what appears to be an initiation chamber for a mystery cult.

The remoteness of the villa is significant. The person who was being initiated was taken away from society to undergo a religious or social transformation so that he or she could be returned to society renewed.

Well-preserved frescoes in vivid colors line the walls of the initiation chamber. When interpreted in sequence, they offer an insight into initiation ceremonies of the classical world. Historians argue that the ceremony depicted in the frescoes is part of a tribal religion. Although there are various interpretations of its details, experts agree on some key points. Based around the mysteries of the cult of Dionysus, the Greek wine god (known as Bacchus to the Romans), the rites played out in the frescoes are intended to prepare young girls for the psychological transition to womanhood and life as a married woman.

The fact that the male figure at the center of the frescoes is Dionysus (Bacchus) is significant. He was the most popular god for Roman women, since he represented a source of sensual and spiritual hope for women in a largely male-dominated society.

Dionysus was also said to symbolize the process of life, death, and rebirth. The initiation ceremony sets out to instill in the female initiate a sense of purpose and security in attaining womanhood. Through this new sense of purpose, the aim of the ceremony was to diminish the initiate's fear of death.

Below: This photograph shows the frescoes from the Villa of the Mysteries that survived the volcanic eruption of 79 CE.

Right: This detail from the frescoes at the Villa of the Mysteries shows a woman and a child being initiated into the cult of Bacchus (Dionysus).

The Orphic Mysteries paid tribute to the poet and prophet for whom they were named—Orpheus. These rites, too, are poorly documented: they seem to have involved symbolic representations of death and rebirth.

The Greeks and Romans also adopted preexisting rites in honor of the Egyptian goddess Isis, transforming her cult into a mystery of the Mother Goddess (see box, page 931). The Anatolian goddess Cybele, also known as Magna Mater ("Great Mother"), together with her son/lover Attis, became the focus of a mystery cult when her worship was imported to Rome in the second century BCE. The Persian god Mithra, who had been eclipsed by Ahura Mazda under the influence of the Zoroastrian religion, was resurrected as the focus of an all-male initiatory cult that was especially popular with Roman soldiers, to whom he was known as Mithras. Mithraism, already substantially divorced from its Persian roots, became integrated with the Syrian cult of Sol Invictus ("Unconquered Sun"). Even Christianity took on some of the aspects of a mystery religion as it spread. For example, scholars suggest that the manger in which Jesus was born could correspond with the Mithraea—chambers that represented the cave where Roman god Mithras was born.

Although the specifics of most mystery cults are unknown, their ultimate aim was always to help initiates lose their fear of death. The Orphic Mysteries, for example, focused on Orpheus, who descended to Hades to recover his wife Eurydice. Although he was unable to bring her back to the land of the living, he himself had entered the realm of death and returned, and was thus an example to all mortals. The Eleusinian Mysteries were said to culminate in the display of a head of grain, which in some way delivered a message of rebirth, or else one of an assured and happy afterlife for the initiates.

The rise of Christianity and the demise of the cults

As Christianity spread it replaced mystery cults. Although the cults were exclusive—only members could take part— for hundreds of years they had all coexisted without conflict. Christianity, on the other hand, was a religion that had no truck with other faiths. The Christian belief that there is only one God seemed intolerant and uncivilized to many Greeks and Romans, but the Christian gospel soon spread throughout the northern Mediterranean.

The church prevailed, partly by force of arms and partly also by skillfully grafting itself on to certain pre-Christian

traditions—for example, the old midwinter festival became Christmas. The early church fathers preached not only the divinity of Christ but also that their religion was morally superior to the repellent practices of non-Christians.

Meanwhile the mysteries—which were attractive to anyone who feared death, but which were seldom clear and usually ambivalent about what came after—were sidelined by a religion that made an unequivocal promise to its believers: whoever believes in Jesus Christ as the savior shall be granted eternal life.

LESLIE ELLEN JONES

Bibliography
Graves, Robert. *The Greek Myths*. New York: Penguin USA, 1993.

Turcan, Robert, and Antonia Nevill, trans. *The Cults of the Roman Empire*. Cambridge, MA: Blackwell Publishers, 1996.

SEE ALSO: Crete; Daedalus; Dionysus; Minos; Mithraism; Orpheus; Pasiphae; Poseidon; Zeus.

NARCISSUS

The Greek myth of Narcissus, whose pride caused him to fall in love with his own reflection, has inspired artists and writers since the classical period. Some people have seen the story as a warning against the dangers of vanity; others have viewed the tragedy of Narcissus as the result of his grieving over the death of his sister.

Narcissus was the son of the river god Cephissus and the nymph Liriope; he was born when Cephissus enveloped Liriope in his waters. According to Roman poet Ovid (43 BCE–17 CE), who wrote about Narcissus in *Metamorphoses*, Narcissus's mother was curious to know what sort of life awaited her son. She sought out Tiresias, the blind Greek prophet, and asked him how long Narcissus would live. Tiresias replied vaguely that Narcissus would enjoy a long life if he did not come to know himself. His mother wondered at the meaning of the prophecy, but was encouraged by the prospect of her son thriving to a ripe old age. It was not until Narcissus was 16 years old that his story began to unfold, and his life began to end.

Rejecting suitors

According to Ovid, the adolescent Narcissus was so beautiful that he was constantly fending off the advances of young men and women alike. One maiden in particular was so infatuated with Narcissus that she followed him when he was hunting in a forest. This maiden was the mountain nymph Echo, whom Hera, queen of the Olympians, had punished for distracting her attention with relentless conversation while her husband Zeus conducted one of his love affairs. Hera's punishment was for Echo always to have the last word, but never the first—all the nymph could do was repeat the words of others.

As she followed Narcissus on his hunt, Echo's passion grew stronger and stronger, as did her desire to reveal herself to the youth. When Narcissus became separated from his fellow hunters, Echo began to move among the shadows of the forest. Aware he was being watched, Narcissus called out, "Is there anyone there?" Echo, however, could only repeat his last words, and this exchange continued until he beckoned her out of the woods. When she tried to run into his arms, he resisted her advances, saying that he would rather die than let her possess him. Humiliated and hurt, Echo retreated into the hollows of the mountains and never showed her face again. Only her voice remained, which, for Greeks and Romans, served as an explanation of the echoes they heard in hills and valleys.

Condemned to self-love

While some suggest that it was Narcissus's rejection of Echo that brought about his fate, others claim that his treatment of Echo was part of a pattern the arrogant youth had established with previous suitors. He had scorned so many potential lovers that one of them, in a moment of vindictiveness, prayed that Narcissus might fall in love and not be able to possess the object of his desires. According to Ovid, this prayer was answered by Nemesis, the goddess of retribution. In other versions, the deity was the virgin goddess Artemis. Either way, the prayer was answered: while Narcissus rested by a pool to quench his thirst, he caught sight of his own reflection and was so captivated by it that he tried to embrace it. After trying repeatedly to grasp the image in his arms, he began to weep, but his tears only created ripples in the pool, thus hampering his efforts to see his own reflection. He ripped open his shirt and began to beat his chest in frustration and anguish. Narcissus was doomed, since he could not tear himself away from the image he saw in the pool. As he wasted away with longing he repeatedly cried, "Alas!" Echo, who was nearby, echoed his anguish with her own voice. At last Narcissus died, but even as his spirit made its way to the underworld it was fixated on its own reflection in the waters of the Styx River.

Not everyone agreed with Ovid's version of the myth. For example, Greek travel writer Pausanias (143–176 CE) maintained in his *Description of Greece* that the idea of Narcissus falling in love with himself was absurd. Instead, Pausanias suggested that the reflection that Narcissus

Above: This painting of Narcissus gazing at his own reflection is by Italian artist Caravaggio (1573–1610).

saw in the pool reminded him of his dead twin sister, whom he adored.

When Narcissus died, his sisters—water nymphs known as Naiads—began preparing for his funeral, but they found in place of his body the yellow-and-white flower of a plant in the amaryllis family that became known as the narcissus in his memory. The flower, one of the earliest to bloom in spring, has a head that points slightly downward, as if Narcissus himself were still pining away, gazing at himself in the pool (see box, page 936).

Flora and Fauna in Greek Myth

Just as the ancient Greeks and Romans developed stories to explain natural phenomena such as thunder—they believed that Zeus's weapon was the thunderbolt—so their myths explained the origins of different plants and animals. Ovid's *Metamorphoses*, which can be translated as "transformations," is a comprehensive collection of such explanatory myths. While many of Ovid's tales highlight the transformations of mythological characters such as Narcissus, who displeased the gods, the poet also treated his audiences to more compassionate myths. For example, when the youth Hyacinthus was accidentally killed, the god Apollo, who loved him, transformed him into the hyacinth flower. Another deity who fell in love with a mortal was the goddess Aphrodite, who pined for the beautiful boy Adonis. When Adonis died, Aphrodite caused the anemone flower to spring up from the drops of his blood. Ovid also included stories of couples whose love was commemorated in nature, such as the minstrel Orpheus, whose love for Eurydice survived in the song of the nightingales at the foot of Mount Olympus, and the elderly couple Baucis and Philemon, who were spared death by being transformed into intertwining oak and linden trees.

Right: Like other members of the plant genus Narcissus, *the daffodil appears to look downward, as if contemplating its reflection.*

Interpretations and inspiration

As well as explaining the origins of the narcissus flower, the story of Narcissus perhaps served as a warning to Greek and Roman people that vanity and self-absorption were not characteristics that befitted members of their societies. Another, related suggestion is that the story owed much to the ancient Greek superstition that it was unlucky to look at one's own reflection. In the modern era, Narcissus has provided a name for a psychological condition. A person who has an excessive degree of self-esteem or self-absorption, and is thus unable to identify with the feelings of others, is often diagnosed with narcissistic personality disorder, or narcissism. The condition was first named by Sigmund Freud (1856–1939), Austrian neurologist and the founder of psychoanalysis, who believed that many classical myths provided insights into human psychology.

The story of Narcissus's demise has also served as inspiration for English poets Geoffrey Chaucer (c. 1342–1400), Edmund Spenser (1552–1599), John Milton (1608–1674), Percy Bysshe Shelley (1792–1822), and John Keats (1795–1821). Among the numerous paintings that depict Narcissus are nearly 50 murals found on the walls of houses excavated in the Roman city of Pompeii—which was buried in ash after a volcanic eruption in 79 CE—and works by Nicolas Poussin (1594–1665), Elihu Vedder (1836–1923), John William Waterhouse (1849–1917), and Salvador Dali (1904–1989). As a trait in people, narcissism was satirized in the 18th century in a comic play entitled *Narcissism, or The Self Admirer* by Swiss philosopher Jean-Jacques Rousseau (1712–1778). The story of Echo and Narcissus also inspired a poem by French writer Jean Cocteau (1889–1963), which in turn formed the basis for the ballet *Le Jeune Homme et la Mort* (The Young Man and Death) by French choreographer Roland Petit (b. 1924).

DEBORAH THOMAS

Bibliography

Ovid, and A. D. Melville, trans. *Metamorphoses.* New York: Oxford University Press, 1998.
Pausanias, and Peter Levi, trans. *Guide to Greece.* New York: Viking Press, 1984.

SEE ALSO: Adonis; Aphrodite; Artemis; Echo; Hera; Nemesis; Orpheus; Zeus.

NATIVE AMERICANS

The pre-Christian religions of the Native Americans were polytheistic, with divine spirits representing various aspects of nature, human characteristics, land, space, and time. Although in many ways every Native American grouping may be said to have had its own unique religion, some general themes are common to most of their belief systems.

Below: Native Americans of the Pacific Northwest believed that lunar eclipses occurred when the moon was swallowed by a sky monster. This photograph from 1915 depicts the ceremonial dance that was performed in order to make it disgorge its prey.

Numerous Native American religious systems shared a belief in harmony among all elements of existence. Their rituals reflected the peoples' sense of oneness with their surroundings. For example, the drum music and many of the ceremonial dances, chants, and songs of the Great Plains Indians were inspired by their veneration of horses, and many of their sacred rituals described buffalo hunts, on which they depended for food. Similarly, Alaskan and Pacific Northwestern religions focused on the ways in which the indigenous peoples acquired their food: by sea fishing, seal hunting, ice fishing, running salmon, and harvesting shellfish.

Although Native Americans saw divinity in all things, many specific geographic locations were identified as being particularly sacred. One of the most notable sites was Celilo Falls, which was destroyed in 1957 by the construction of the Dalles Dam on the Columbia River in Oregon. Celilo Falls was an ancient place of worship for Pacific Northwest Indians, including the Umatilla, Nez Percé, Yakima, and

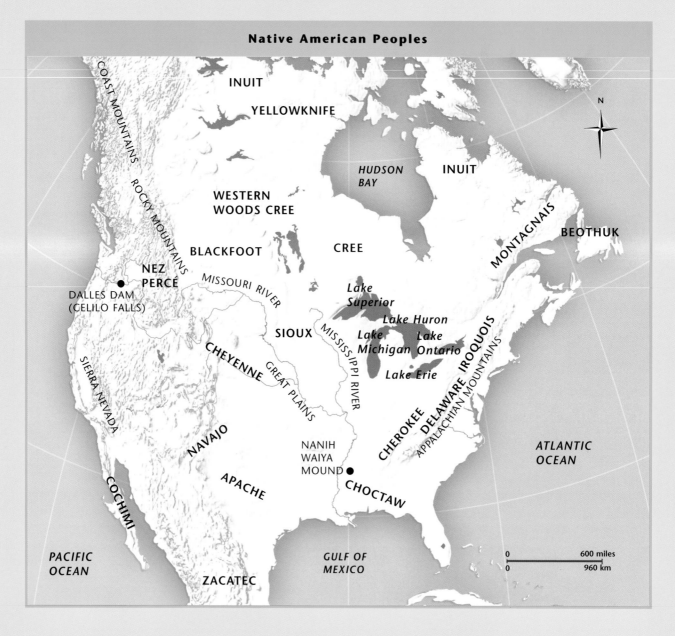

Native American Peoples

Warm Springs Indians. Among the ceremonies they performed there were the First Food Observances, during which the salmon, led by Coyote, a powerful spirit entity, swam upriver to spawn in the spring. Like all pre-Christian Native American myths, this legend was transmitted by oral tradition.

Explaining natural harmony

The general subject of most Native American myths was interaction between spirits that explained some aspect of natural harmony or why certain practices ensured harmony. Others were descriptive narratives that explained fundamental beliefs about the world and humans' place in it.

The Iroquois of the northeast recognized many spirit entities. One of the most important was Hahgwehdiyu, who gave the people their staple food by planting a grain of maize in the body of his mother, Atahensic. In some myths Hahgwehdiyu was pitted against his twin brother Hahgwehdaetgah, who was an evil spirit. Ioskeha was an Iroquois creator spirit who brought to life the first man and woman. Ioskeha defeated demons, healed diseases, and gave tobacco to the Iroquois, who used it as a ritual herb. Another Iroquois creation myth attributed the formation of the Five Nations—Mohawk, Oneida, Seneca, Cayuga, and Onondaga—to Tarhuhiawahku, a sky spirit. Long ago, according to the legend, Tarhuhiawahku created people. He called them together and said: "I give corn to the Mohawks. I give nuts and fruit of many trees to the patient Oneidas. I give beans to the industrious Senecas. I give roots of plants to eat to the friendly Cayugas. I give grapes and squashes to eat, and tobacco to smoke at camp-fires, to the wise and eloquent Onondagas." Finally, Tarhuhiawahku

Some Major Deities of Native American Peoples

Asgaya Gigagei: Cherokee thunder god.

Atahensic: Iroquois sky goddess, mother of Hahgwehdiyu and Hahgwehdaetgah.

Atius Tirawa: Pawnee creator deity.

Awonawilona (All-Container): Pueblo Zuni creator deity.

Changing Woman: Principal Navajo creator deity.

Coyote: Powerful trickster spirit of the Umatilla, Nez Percé, and Yakima who stole fire from the spirits.

Ga-gaah (Wise Crow): Divine bird of the Iroquois who brought corn to humankind.

Geezhigo-Quae: Delaware sky mother.

Glooskap: Good Algonquian creator deity, son of Nokomis.

Hahgwehdaetgah: Iroquois evil spirit, twin brother of Hahgwehdiyu.

Hahgwehdiyu: Iroquois creator spirit; provider of food.

Hisakitaimisi (Master of Breath): Supreme deity of the Cree.

Ioskeha: Principal creator spirit of the Iroquois.

Kana'ti (Lucky Hunter): Cherokee hunter deity.

Kuloskap: Creator deity of the Micmac and Passamaquoddy.

Malsum: Evil Algonquian creator deity, son of Nokomis and brother of Glooskap.

Masewi and Oyoyewa: Pueblo divine twin brothers, who placed the sun in the sky.

Monster Slayer and Child-of-Water: Navajo warrior deities, twin sons of Changing Woman.

Nokomis (Grandmother): Algonquian earth goddess.

Running Antelope: Otoe human spirit who became the man in the moon.

Selu (Corn): Cherokee deity who created corn.

Sila or Silap Inua: Inuit creator deity and divine ruler.

Skookums: Evil monster spirits of the Pacific Northwest Peoples. The Skookums guarded the fire that Coyote stole.

Wakan Tanka: Sioux spirit entity, the sum of all Wakan spirits.

White Buffalo Calf Woman: Sioux goddess of pipe smoking.

gave knowledge to all the Five Nations, then wrapped himself in a bright cloud and went away "like a swift arrow into the sun." In some myths, Tuscaroras were named as the sixth Iroquois nation: they went up the Roanoke River, where Tarhuhiawahku lived among them and taught them arts and crafts. The Tuscaroras claimed that this direct contact with the deity made them superior to other Iroquois nations.

Great spirits

Many Native Americans, including the Anishinabe of the eastern and midwestern Great Lakes and the Leni Lenape of the Midwest, believed in manitous, or great spirit entities, which they worshiped with prayer and offerings. For the Leni Lenape (also known as the Delaware), an important female manitou was Geezhigo-Quae (sky mother). Several myths related her creation of the world and humanity. She was said to have plunged into the primal waters to find land, and from it fashioned the earth's hills, valleys, and mountains. Manitous often taught humans traditional hunting, gathering, and fishing methods. One Anishinabe group, the Ojibwa of the Great Lakes region, traditionally practiced spearfishing at night. The myth of how they learned to fish helped to explain the dynamics of nocturnal spearfishing in springtime. A young boy, Winaboozhoo, was taught to spear walleyes at night by an old, partly blind Indian, who was himself a manitou, or supernatural spirit. The old man had developed nocturnal spearfishing techniques because he could easily see the large eyes of the walleye shine in the light of his flaming torch. The old man taught the boy all that he knew, and in return Winaboozhoo promised never to take more fish than

Above: In this photograph from 1926 a Pueblo of the American Southwest places a feather at the foot of a waterfall as an offering to the cloud gods.

he could eat. Thus the manitou would never go hungry and the balance of nature would be maintained. Winaboozhoo passed his newly acquired skill on to his people, and they agreed to honor his pact with the old man. This myth describes a negotiation between human and spirit worlds, and explains how a subsistence tradition was given to humans by a manitou, to be passed down through generations.

Algonquian-speaking Indians of the northeast believed in Nokomis (grandmother), an earth goddess who fed plants, animals, and people. In this she was similar to a manitou. One of the most important Algonquian myths concerned Nokomis's sons, Glooskap and Malsum. Glooskap was good, wise, and creative; Malsum was evil,

Birth of the Supreme Deity of the Algonquians

In the beginning, an old woman lived on an island in a tepee with her only daughter. Every day the old woman went out alone to gather wild potatoes. One day her daughter begged to go with her, and the two set out. They came to the damp ravine where the old woman usually dug. She warned her daughter to face southward. The girl promised to do so and happily set to work. As time went by, however, she forgot her promise. She looked northward, and suddenly a great rushing, roaring noise came from the heavens; the wind swept down and whirled her round and round. Just as suddenly, the wind stopped, and the air calmed. The two women quickly gathered up their potatoes and went home. After that experience, the old woman worked alone. The daughter later gave birth to three children: the first was Manabozho; the second was a little wolf, Muh'wäse; and the last was a sharp flint stone, which cut her. She died from the resulting wound. The old woman mourned her daughter, and in rage and grief, she threw away the flint stone. She cherished Manabozho and Muh'wäse, and cared for them until they grew to be adults. Manabozho became the supreme manitou of Algonquian-speaking peoples of north and northeastern North America. Many myths described his exploits: he created the world, he created humans, and he played games such as lacrosse. Several myths pair him with his wolf-brother—they ruled either as joint or opposing forces.

selfish, and destructive. When Nokomis died, Glooskap created good plants, animals, and humans from his mother's body, while Malsum made poisonous plants and snakes. Glooskap created many wonderful things, but Malsum grew tired of his brother's goodness and decided to kill him. In an attempt to trick Glooskap into revealing his weakness, Malsum bragged that he himself could not be harmed by anything except the roots of a fern plant, which could kill him. He pestered Glooskap for days in order to find out his good brother's weak spot. Glooskap finally confided that he could be killed by an owl feather. As soon as Malsum heard this, he made a dart with an owl feather and killed Glooskap. However, the power of good was stronger than evil, and Glooskap rose from the dead. Glooskap now had no choice but to destroy Malsum so that good could prevail. He went to a stream and loudly declared that a reed could also kill him. Malsum came immediately, intent on killing him again. Glooskap pulled a fern plant up by the roots and flung it at Malsum, who fell down dead. Malsum's spirit went underground and became a wicked wolf spirit that feared the light of day but surfaced occasionally to torment humans and animals.

The land of the Choctaw

Choctaw myths describe how the people came to their promised land of Mississippi, and how the sacred Naniah Waiya Mound was formed. Two brothers, Chata and Chicksah, led the Original People from a land in the far west. They traveled a long time, guided by a magic pole. Every night when they camped, they placed the pole in the ground, and each morning they set off in the direction in which the pole leaned. Eventually, after traveling a vast distance, they came to a place where the pole remained upright. In a cave there they laid to rest their ancestors' bones, which they had carried in buffalo sacks from their homeland. Naniah Waiya Mound grew from that mass burial pile.

Eventually Chata and Chicksah realized that the new land could not support all their followers. Chicksah took half of them and traveled to the north; they became the Chickasaw. Chata and the others remained near the sacred mound and were known as the Choctaw. To this day, Choctaw elders claim that the ground near the mound and cave are sacred. Choctaw believe that they will die if they are away from their sacred land too long.

Right: Native Americans respected all animals, but the Sioux particularly venerated the rare white buffalo.

Sioux White Buffalo Calf Woman

Many Native American myths describe the origin and explain the meaning of ritual ceremonies. An outstanding example is the story of White Buffalo Calf Woman, which provided the background for almost the whole mythology of the Lakota Sioux of the Midwest and West. The legend concerns two men on a hunting trip who saw a beautiful young woman dressed in white buckskin. One of the men had evil thoughts about her; the other man warned him that she was probably *wakan* (a sacred spirit). The first man did not heed the warning: he approached her and was surrounded by a white mist. When the mist lifted, only his skeleton remained. The woman then went to the other man's village. She told the people that she came from heaven to teach them how to live and to predict their

Kana'ti and Selu

One of the most vivid myths of the Cherokee concerns Kana'ti (Lucky Hunter) and Selu (Corn), who lived with their only child, a boy. Kana'ti always brought home game animals, which Selu washed in the river. The little boy played by the river every day. He said another boy came out of the water and called himself Elder Brother. The parents knew that the strange boy had sprung from the blood of the game. They adopted Elder Brother. He had magical powers, and they called him I'nage-utasvhi (He-who-grew-up-wild); he remained wild and led his brother in mischief. The brothers were responsible for the hardships that humans have to face while growing food and hunting game. The brothers discovered that Selu was a witch who could magically produce corn. In fear, they killed her, but before her death she told them to clear a large plot to grow corn. The boys cleared only seven little spots. Thus, corn grows only in a few places instead of all over the earth. The brothers discovered that Kana'ti kept all animals and birds in a cave on a mountain. The brothers removed the rock that blocked the entrance to the cave, and released all the animals and birds: forevermore, humans must hunt for game. After the boys released the animals and birds, Kana'ti went into the cave and kicked open four jars: out swarmed bedbugs, fleas, lice, and gnats, which attacked the boys and forever after harassed humans.

Left: This sand painting by a Navajo artist depicts one of the powerful and mysterious Yei deities.

future. She gave the people maize. She taught them about a sacred pipe and explained its significance. Its bowl represented earth, its stem represented plants, the buffalo calf carved on it represented animals, and the 12 eagle feathers that decorated it represented flying creatures. She taught the Sioux to pray with the pipe, and promised that those who did so would join with all life in the universe. She revealed to them a sacred stone carved with seven circles, one for each of seven sacred ceremonies. She taught them the first of these, the Ghost Keeping Ceremony, and foretold that the other six would be revealed in due course. The Ghost Keeping Ceremony ensured that a departed soul would return to Wakan Tanka (great spirit or creator).

In the ceremony, a sacred bundle was made of sweet grass and a lock of the deceased's hair. The bundle, kept for a year in a sacred place, was prayed to incessantly. Finally the soul would be released through ritual prayers, purification rites, and offerings. The woman then gave the Lakota four colors that represented the four main winds; she illustrated them by turning herself first into a white buffalo calf, then a black one, then a red one, and last a yellow one. Then she disappeared. Henceforth she was known to the Sioux as White Buffalo Calf Woman.

The Changing Woman

The Navajo of the Southwest, who called themselves the Dineh ("the people"), worshiped powerful and mysterious deities known as Yei ("holy people"). The deities included Changing Woman, Sun, Earth, Moon, Sky, Talking God, Child-of-Water, Monster Slayer, Thunders, Winds, and Failed-to-Speak People. The Dineh were a matrilineal society, and the principal deity was Changing Woman, often referred to as the mother of the people. Changing Woman was the first entity to give physical birth; her husband, Sun, impregnated her and she delivered twin boys, Monster Slayer and Child-of-Water. She created Earth Surface People, ancestors of the Dineh. All of the Yei made masks of themselves out of white beads, turquoise, abalone, and jet. They directed humans to reproduce these masks on buckskin painted white, blue, red, and black. These masks were worn in ritual dances and ceremonies, such as the Blessing Way rites taught to the Dineh by Changing Woman. Blessing Way rites were fundamental to the Dineh religion and governed their entire chant system of ceremonial cures, which maintained harmony, brought good luck, averted misfortune, invoked blessings for protection and childbirth, increased possessions, and consecrated objects and marriages. Blessing Way rites included ritual baths, songs, prayers, sand paintings, hogan (house) consecration, body blessing, traditional storytelling, and inhaling the dawn air. Pollen was used to anoint everything involved in the ceremonies, including objects, participants, and spectators.

Horse-and-buffalo cultures

The societies of Native Americans of the Great Plains are sometimes described as horse-and-buffalo cultures because they were founded on riding the former in pursuit of the latter. One of their most famous myths, the Legend of the Buffalo Dance, belonged to the Siksika ("those with black moccasins"), more commonly known as the Blackfeet of Montana and Canada. The story concerned the practice of driving buffalo herds over cliffs. The Siksika had to eat buffalo in order to survive, but their belief in harmonious existence and the oneness of all things created a tension between their sacred tenets and their need to slaughter great animals for food. The Legend of the Buffalo Dance explained the sanctity of cliff-hunting and offered a way of resolving this conflict.

Long ago, the cliff-hunts failed and the people were hungry. One morning, a young Siksika woman looked up a cliff and saw a herd of grazing buffalo. She cried out: "If you will only jump into our corral down here, I shall marry one of you!" The buffalo hurtled over the cliff, and one big bull demanded marriage. He pointed out that the corral was full of hides and meat for her people.

Right: Worshiping buffalo and hunting them for food were not contradictory aims for the Plains peoples. As long as no one killed too many animals, the balance of nature would be maintained.

The woman kept her word, and went off with him across the prairie. Her father searched for her, and a magpie helped him find her. Her buffalo husband and the other bulls then killed the father. They trampled him under their hooves, hooked him with their horns, and trampled him again until there was nothing left of him. The woman mourned and wailed. Her buffalo husband reproached her, reminding her of all the buffalo that her people had killed in cliff-hunts—they, too, were mourned by their buffalo relatives. However, he took pity on his wife and told her that if she could restore her father to life, she and her father could return to their people. The magpie helped the woman find a piece of her father in the trampled earth. She placed it on the ground, covered it with her robe, and sang a certain song. She then removed the robe and saw her father's re-formed body lying there. She covered it with the robe and resumed her song. When

Above: A Native American Algonquian hunter is depicted blowing smoke into the mouth of a bear he has just killed in order to make peace with its spirit.

she removed the robe again, her father breathed and stood up. Her buffalo husband was amazed and recognized her holy power. He taught the woman the buffalo dance and song by which the animals would be restored to life when her people slaughtered them for food, just as her own father had been restored. The buffalo would not really die, but would live on after the Siksika had "borrowed" their hides and meat. The Buffalo Dance ritual continued among the Siksika in a male-only society known as I-kun-uh'-kah-tsi ("all comrades"), until the "iron horse" (railroad locomotive) cut across the prairies, the buffalo were wiped out, and the hunters became farmers or laborers.

The hunters' concern for the hunted

Reconciling the need to kill animals for food with the need to live harmoniously with nature was a challenge for Native Americans and was often discussed in myths. Animals were believed to have spirits similar to human

spirits, and myths often described how animals perceived and related to humans. A myth common to many Native American peoples revealed contact between humans and animals that resulted in "the coming of medicine." A long time ago, people and animals lived together in peace and harmony, but this changed when greedy people began to hunt not just for food to eat, but to sell meat and fur. The animal population dwindled, and the animals were worried. White Bear called a council of animals to decide upon a method of revenge. The oldest and wisest fly suggested that they ask the spirits to create diseases that the animals could carry to the humans. Thus, a great sickness spread through all Native American villages, afflicting everyone. The animals, saddened because they had only wanted to punish the bad people, called another council to discuss the problem. The herbs promised to heal the sick, so the animals sent spirit dreams to all the shamans, the peoples' intermediaries with the spirit world, to guide them to the herbs: thus, healing medicine was brought to the Native Americans.

Several Native American peoples from the Pacific Northwest—including the Karok, Clatsop, Yakima, Nez Percé, Wasco, Warm Springs, Coos, Umpqua, Coquille,

Spirit of the Inuit

In addition to its literal meaning, "person," the word *Inua* (or *yua*) was used by Inuit (Aleuts) to convey the concept of spirit. *Inua* resided in objects, people, animals, and geographic features. For example, the *inua* of a seal was not just the *inua* of that particular seal but also of the entire species. Sila, also known as Silap Inua, was the divine ruler of the Inuit. Sila was a force that permeated the universe, nature, the winds, and the weather: it was the air that people breathed, and the energy that moved everything, collectively and separately. Sila was a creator deity who was responsible for forming the earth and sky. Sila ruled air and light and had the power to create earthquakes. The Inuit belief in Sila was responsible for their worldview that all things were inextricably linked and equal—humans were no more important than animals; rather, they all shared equal status and the same spiritual continuity. Continuity and harmony could be maintained only if animals and humans thought and behaved rightly. Seals "acted rightly" in allowing humans to kill them for food, and humans "acted rightly" in "keeping the thoughts of the seals" in their own minds. "Keeping the thoughts of the seals" allowed a way or path for seal inua to enter human life safely and honorably during the hunt. In the same way, a pregnant woman "acted rightly" by thinking constantly of her unborn child's inua, thus preparing a path for the baby's safe delivery and growth in the human world.

Right: The main carving on this Inuit knife handle depicts a seal coming up for air. The Inuit depended on seals for food.

Klamath, Shasta, and Modoc—had a common myth to explain the origin of fire. In the beginning, people had no fire. Fire was guarded by three old skookums (evil spirits) on a mountaintop. The people had no heat in their homes and ate their salmon raw, so they begged wise Coyote for help. Coyote and his three sisters, who lived as huckleberries in his stomach, formulated a plan to steal fire. Coyote knew the skookums could run fast despite their great age, so he planned to pass the stolen fire down the mountain to the people below in a relay of all the animals. Coyote stole the fire, and a skookum grabbed Coyote's tail as he passed it to Cougar: Coyote's tail was black-tipped ever after. Cougar passed fire to Fox; Fox passed it to Squirrel, whose tail was also caught by a skookum: thereafter Squirrel's tail always curled upward. Squirrel passed fire to Antelope, the fastest of all animals. Antelope got a long way ahead of the skookum and fire passed from animal to animal until it dwindled to a hot

coal and was passed to Frog. Frog swallowed the hot coal and hopped off as fast as he could, but the skookums caught up with him. The youngest skookum caught Frog's tail and severed it: forevermore, Frog had no tail. Frog swam across a river, followed by the skookums. Exhausted, Frog spat the hot coal onto Wood, and Wood swallowed it. The skookums were mystified by this turn of events—they did not know how to get fire back out of Wood—and so they returned sadly to their mountaintop. Wise Coyote taught the people how to get fire out of Wood by rubbing two sticks together. Ever since, people have had fire to cook their salmon and heat their homes.

How the man got into the moon

One of many Native American myths that endeavor to explain natural phenomena is the story of how the man got into the moon, told by the Otoe people of the Midwest. A youth named Running Antelope lived with

Left: Modern Native Americans wearing traditional costumes dance in Grand Prairie, Texas. Such re-creations help to maintain traditional rituals.

and Running Antelope fled. The chief chased after him, shooting poisoned arrows at him as they ran. Almost overtaken, Running Antelope came to the sandy bank of a lake. He prayed to the water spirits for salvation and jumped into the lake. The water spirits hurled Running Antelope all the way to the moon on a great swirling geyser of water. Running Antelope became the Man in the Moon. Although he had been saved from the chief, he was forever separated from his wife.

Native American religion in the modern world

Native American mythology was a complex fusion between natural and supernatural worlds. The overall principle of harmony among human, natural, and supernatural powers was common to all Native American belief systems. Today, although most Native Americans are Christian, many groups have revived their traditional beliefs and resumed ancient ceremonies, dances, chants, songs, and the ceremonial use of tobacco and peyote. Ancient myths are still passed down by word of mouth from parent to child in a continuation of an age-old oral tradition, thus keeping alive the power of the spirits that have governed Native Americans since before recorded history. In the latter part of the 20th century, ancient Native American ideas of universal harmony fired the imaginations of some European Americans, who adopted them in their search for an alternative lifestyle.

ALYS CAVINESS

his grandmother in a circular village in the mountains. Running Antelope went to visit a prairie village, whose chief was very cruel. The cruel chief loved a beautiful maiden named Little Hill, but was unable to win her affection. Running Antelope and Little Hill fell in love: they married, and lived in her village. The chief was angry and threatened to take Little Hill away from Running Antelope. Almost every night, when people gathered for games and entertainment, the chief tried to win her affection. He cast beautiful pieces of coral, turquoise, and beads onto the ground for the people, hoping that Little Hill would love him for his generosity. One night Running Antelope went home, but Little Hill was not there. Running Antelope stealthily went to the chief's lodge and heard the voice of Little Hill singing. He burst into the lodge and demanded his wife. The chief pulled a knife

Bibliography

Anderson, Bernice G. *Indian Sleep Man Tales: Authentic Legends of the Otoe Tribe.* Caldwell, ID: Caxton Printers, Ltd., 1940.

Cooper, J. C. *Symbolic and Mythological Animals.* New York: HarperCollins, 1992.

Grinnell, George Bird. *Blackfoot Lodge Tales: The Story of a Prairie People.* Lincoln, NE: University of Nebraska Press, 1962.

Hirschfelder, Arlene, and Paulette Molin. *Encyclopedia of Native American Religions.* New York: Checkmark Books, 2000.

Jaimes, M. Annette, ed. *The State of Native America.* Boston: South End Press, 1992.

Nesper, Larry. *The Walleye War.* Lincoln. NE: University of Nebraska Press, 2002.

Sullivan, Lawrence E., ed. *Native Religions and Cultures of North America, Anthropology of the Sacred.* New York: Continuum, 2000.

SEE ALSO: Animals; Animal Worship; Creation Myths; Great Spirit; Natural Forces; Nature Religions; Polytheism; Shamans.

NATURAL FORCES

Early peoples did not understand the causes of natural forces such as earthquakes, winds, storms, floods, and volcanoes, so they invented myths to explain them.

Most early peoples believed that the earth was fixed in space, and that the sun, moon, and stars revolved around it. The earth was founded on some support, and earthquakes occurred when that support moved. In ancient Japan the support was believed to be a great spider, and later a giant catfish. In Mongolia and Celebes (modern Sulawesi, an island between Indonesia and the Philippines), it was believed to be a hog; in India, a huge mole; in parts of South America, a whale; and among some Native American peoples, a giant tortoise. Some mythologies told of a giant in human form who supported the earth or the sky. The Maya believed that the earth was flat with four corners, at each of which there was a bacab (jaguar) of a different color that held up the sky.

In some ancient cultures the earth itself was believed to have been created from the dismembered limbs of a sacrificial deity, such as the Hindu Prajapati in India, or from an earlier mother goddess who had been downgraded to monster status. An example of the latter is the Babylonian dragon Tiamat, which was slain by Marduk. The mountains and hills were often said to have been formed from piles of the bodies of earlier beings. The giants killed by the Navajo hero Monster Slayer are one example; the Norse myth in which the god Odin and his brothers Vili and Vé created the world from the body of the giant Ymir is another.

Shaking the foundations

In many cultures earthquakes were thought to come from a stumble, spasm, or some other movement by the gods or animals carrying the earth on their shoulders. In Samoa, for example, the god holding up the earth was warned by his people not to move too much lest the earth fall apart. One belief from Celebes said that grass was the hog god's hair. When the earth shook, they pulled out bunches of it in an effort to make him stop moving. The Shan people of

Below: Tornadoes, like this one photographed in Oklahoma, were one of the many terrifying displays of natural power that gave rise to myths.

Earthquakes in the Teutonic World

In Nordic-Germanic mythology, earth's underworld caverns are filled with the smithies of dwarves and giants crafting magical works at their forges. Sometimes their intense subterranean activity causes earthquakes. In addition to these smiths, there are also tremors caused as a routine side-effect of the punishment of Loki, the trickster god, who is held securely bound, face upward, while a serpent's venom drips toward him. His wife Sigyn catches the venom in a bowl, but whenever she has to leave to empty it the poison falls into the face of the anguished Loki. His writhings are felt as earthquakes on the surface.

Burma believed that a big fish slept beneath the earth. When it accidentally bit its own tail, pain abruptly awoke it, and its movements were felt as an earthquake. Seismic tremors might also be caused by a god personifying earth who turns over in his sleep—in Fiji, people made sacrifices to their slumbering earth god so that he would turn over gently and not hurt them.

In other cultures there are deities who can use earthquakes as punishment. Poseidon, Greek god of the sea, caused earthquakes to take revenge on those who had angered him. In the Book of Isaiah in the Old Testament of the Judeo-Christian Bible, God promises that earthquakes, tempests, and devouring fires will scatter his people's foes. In the New Testament, one earthquake parts the veil of the temple immediately after Christ's death, and another comes as divine intervention to break open the doors of the cell in which Paul and Silas are imprisoned. In Revelation, the final, prophetic, book of the New Testament, it is predicted that earthquakes will accompany the opening of the sixth and seventh seals. In Norse tradition, earthquakes will announce the Twilight of the Gods and the uprooting of every tree except the World Tree.

Winds of change

Air movement was another natural phenomenon that the ancients found inexplicable in rational terms. According to Greek poet Hesiod (fl. 800 BCE), the four main mild winds—Boreas (north), Eurus (east), Notus (south), and Zephyrus (west)—were sent by the gods as blessings. All other winds were produced by the hideous winged monster Typhon, whose head touched the skies, whose outstretched arms spanned the sky, whose huge hands were augmented by a hundred dragon heads, and whose body was covered with hissing snakes.

Destructive winds have different names, depending on where in the world they occur. As a class, they may all be termed *cyclones*, an English word derived from the Greek word *kykloun*, meaning "to circle around" or "to whirl." Names for these circular storms, however, are often interchangeable. If a tropical cyclone in the Atlantic Ocean or the Gulf of Mexico builds into a storm of severe intensity, it becomes known as a hurricane, named for Huracan, the ancient Mayan god of whirlwinds and thunderstorms. Huracan is reputed to have created earth by chanting "Earth, earth, earth" repeatedly into the primal seas until solid land arose with a multitude of life-forms,

Right: This statue depicts the Aztec god Tonatiuh. According to Aztec mythology, Tonatiuh presided over an age that would end in a violent earthquake.

Above: Fujin, the Japanese deity depicted in this painting of the 13th century CE, was the god of wind.

including humans. When those first humans offended the gods, Huracan sent a hurricane to destroy his creation.

An Aztec myth also tells of the destruction of the world by a hurricane. In this case the wind god is Quetzalcoatl, the feathered serpent who ruled earth until Tezcatlipoca, a tiger sorcerer-god from an earlier world, reached up with his paw and pulled him from the skies. The violent impact of Quetzalcoatl's fall created a devastating hurricane that destroyed all plant life and all but a few humans, who were turned into monkeys.

The meteorological phenomenon known as a hurricane when it occurs in the Atlantic or Indian Ocean is known as a typhoon when it occurs in the Pacific Ocean or eastern Asian seas. The word is derived partly from the Chinese term *daaih fung* ("big wind"), and partly from an Arabic word that might itself come from the ancient Greek for whirlwind, *typhon*, named for the wind monster Typhon.

In European myth, witches have the power to raise thunderstorms—the most famous example is that of the three weird sisters in *Macbeth* by William Shakespeare (1564–1616). Among Old World thunder gods are Baal (Palestine, Phoenicia, and Syria), Jupiter (Rome), Perun

(Russia and Ukraine), Thor (Germany and Scandinavia), Ukko (Finland), and Zeus (Greece). There are also some thunder goddesses. In Japan, for example, Naru-Kami, guardian of trees and artisans, sends lightning and thunderbolts that sanctify whatever soil they strike. In Africa the Yoruba goddess Oya causes and controls thunder and lightning storms on the Niger River. In China, the goddess Tien-Mu flashes two mirrors at each other to create bright, noisy bolts of lightning.

The world's worst winds

Tornadoes are localized hurricanes whose great intensity makes them the most dangerous and destructive of all storms. Native Americans treated them with respect and did what they could to keep out of their way. Unlike immigrant Europeans, they knew better than to erect permanent residences along tornado corridors, such as one in which Oklahoma City now stands. Some Native American peoples see a cleansing, purifying function in

these storms; others see them as punishment from the Great Spirit, although it is the tornadoes themselves, not the humans they visit, that are usually regarded as evil. According to the Papago, or Tohono O'odham, of Arizona, tornadoes cause a dizzy sickness. In New Mexico, the Zuni believe that witches travel in tornadoes, while the Jemez blame such storms for causing miscarriages. Among Native American peoples of California and as far west as Hawaii, tornadoes are thought to contain poison, evil spirits, or the dust of dead shamans. They can cause nightmares, soul loss, accidents, and even death. The ways to protect oneself from such dangers include throwing water or dirt at the advancing storms, fleeing, hiding, or addressing them directly while at the same time making distracting noises with one's hands and feet. If all else fails, cleansing sage smoke can help to repair any damage.

Flood damage

Stories of a cataclysmic deluge are common in many parts of the world. Of all the major ancient civilizations, Japan and ancient Egypt (along with much of the rest of Africa) are among the few that lack such legends. Scientifically, however, there is no evidence to support the popular claim that there was once a worldwide flood. Even in Mesopotamia (part of modern Iraq), where the flood myth in Hebrew scriptures originated, there is no archaeological evidence for a widespread flood—only two geological sites in the whole region reveal what have been interpreted as

Above: An electrical storm is still an awe-inspiring sight. The power of lightning convinced ancient peoples that it was caused by the gods.

Bringing Lightning Down to Earth

While lightning will always be a frightening phenomenon, people were more afraid of it before they knew what caused it. Many ancient peoples imagined that it was a manifestation of divine wrath. According to Greek legend, Zeus used lightning to influence the outcome of the Trojan War. Egyptians believed that the god Seth created lightning with an iron spear; in Scandinavian myths Thor sent sparks flying when he hurled his hammer earthward. Later, in medieval Europe, people kept pieces of oak in their homes, especially branches from trees that had been struck by lightning, in the belief that the species would draw lightning to itself. Eventually, acorns replaced the branches. Vestiges of this tradition survive in acorn-shaped knobs at the ends of curtain cords. Another medieval superstition was that ringing church bells would disperse lightning. Some medieval church towers even bore the Latin inscription *Fulgura frango* ("I break up lightning"). In the 18th century, scientists discovered that lightning was produced by accumulations of electric charge in the cumulonimbus clouds of thunderstorms. A scientific means of lessening the dangers posed by lightning arrived in 1752 when the lightning rod was invented by Benjamin Franklin (1706–1790).

"flood layers." That is not to deny a possible historical foundation for flood stories such as those of Gilgamesh or Noah's Ark, but suggests that the waters did not cover the entire earth, as implied in the Book of Genesis. Experts believe that the widespread occurrence of deluge stories is based on devastating localized floods—such as one that may have occurred near the Black Sea around 7000 BCE—rather than a single global inundation. These events were mythologized and handed down to succeeding generations. Since most of the world's permanent early human settlements were founded either on the coast or along the banks of rivers, the chances are that most peoples would have had some firsthand experience of floods.

The most famous tidal waves of the ancient world were those that ravaged the Minoan civilization of Crete after a volcanic eruption about 1630 BCE on nearby Thera (modern Santorini). The sudden submergence of most of Thera is thought by many to have inspired myths about Atlantis, a lost continent which, according to Greek philosopher Plato (c. 428–c. 348 BCE), lay beneath the waters of the Atlantic Ocean near the Pillars of Hercules, off Gibraltar. When a volcanic shockwave, tidal waves, and smothering clouds of ash hit Crete, they fatally

Poseidon's "Courtship" Tidal Wave

The Greeks believed the sea god Poseidon was responsible for tidal waves. One of his biggest was the result of a performance staged for Aphrodite's benefit. After the beautiful goddess had emerged from the sea, Zeus promised she could have any husband she wished. Each god immediately began competing for her attentions. Poseidon felt that she already belonged to him because she had arisen from his watery realm. To demonstrate his clear superiority, he commanded a tidal wave to leap as high as Mount Olympus and then to stop just short of flooding the gods' home. It was a dramatic spectacle—the awed gods watched the great wave hovering, curled, over the peak. Then, on Poseidon's command, the wave shrank back into the sea. Aphrodite, however, remained unimpressed. In one version of the myth she eventually married Hephaestus—he offered her exquisite, magical jewelry, which she found more to her taste than displays of water features.

Below: An ancient Roman temple was submerged by flooding along the Black Sea coast of Turkey.

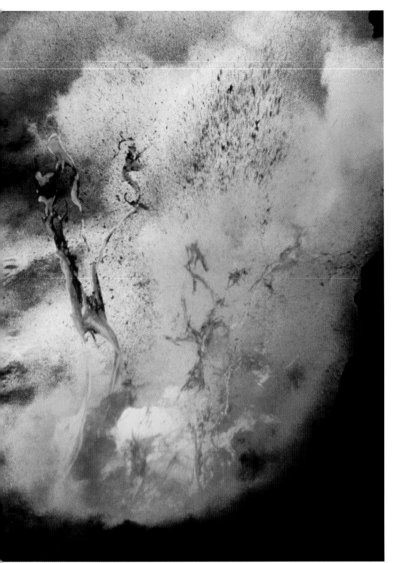

Left: Lava spurts from Mount Kilauea, a volcano on Hawaii that some Hawaiians still say is home to the goddess Pele.

Mount Etna on the island of Sicily. From time to time the fires from Vulcan's forges erupted onto the surface of the earth through volcanoes.

Elsewhere, other explanations exist for volcanic eruptions. In Greek mythology, for example, when Typhon attempted to seize control of Mount Olympus, the chief god, Zeus, angrily smote the usurper with thunderbolts and lightning. Typhon burst into flames and Zeus then imprisoned him in a mountain, where he burned for eternity, from time to time belching fire and molten rocks onto the surface.

In Polynesian mythology, volcanoes are both caused and controlled by the goddess Pele, who is at times depicted as a sensuous maiden, at others as a wily crone, depending on whether the local volcanoes are dormant or erupting. She is particularly important in the myths of Hawaii and Tahiti. Pele is a nature goddess who has the power to create land as well as to destroy it. When she stamps her foot, the earth quakes; when prayed to, she can stop the flow of lava.

According to tradition, Pele was born from the heat of the earth. She was driven out of the western sea by an angry sister, the sea goddess. Finally, she came to live on Hawaii in the volcano of Kilauea. The thin strands of volcanic glass that are drawn out from the molten lava that erupts from Kilauea are known as Pele's hair. Individual strands of this geological material may be less than two hundredths of an inch (0.5 mm) in diameter, but more than 6 feet (2 m) in length. Pele's hair is often blown high into the air by volcanic eruptions.

In ancient Mexico, Mount Popocatépetl was said to have been formed by Aztec gods on the spot where a warrior named Popoca had lain down and died of grief next to the body of his wife, Iztaccíhuatl, who had herself died of a broken heart after hearing false reports of his death in battle. Whenever the volcano erupted, it was said to be a sign that Popoca was still watching over his true love.

KATHLEEN JENKS

Bibliography
Hesiod, and M. L. West, ed. *Theogony; and Works and Days.* New York: Oxford University Press, 1999.
Wyman, Leland Clifton. *The Windways of the Navaho.* Colorado Springs: Taylor Museum of the Colorado Springs Fine Arts Center, 1962.

SEE ALSO: Africa; Atlas; Aztecs; Crete; Loki; Marduk; Maya; Native Americans; Poseidon; Typhon; Zeus.

weakened a 2,000-year-old civilization, which was later taken over by invaders from the Greek mainland.

In Japan, the dragon god of tidal waves was Ryujin, or Luminous Being, who lived at the bottom of the sea. Where the Greek sea god Poseidon used his voice to command the tides, Ryujin achieved the same effect through the use of two magical "tide jewels." He once lent them to a queen heading for battle. As enemy ships were launched, she dropped Low-Tide Jewel into the sea, stranding the entire fleet. As her enemies tried to escape on foot, she dropped High-Tide Jewel; the waters returned suddenly, and all were drowned.

Fire from inside the earth
The English word *volcano* is derived from the name of Vulcan, the blacksmith god of ancient Rome, whose enormous forges were thought to operate full-time under either Mount Vesuvius near Naples on mainland Italy or

NATURE RELIGIONS

Nature religions are different from polytheistic systems, such as those of the ancient Greeks and Romans, in which there are many gods. They are also quite unlike the great monotheistic religions of Judaism, Christianity, and Islam, in which everything is believed to have been created and ordered by one almighty god. Adherents of nature religions believe that there is a divinity or a spirit in every creature, every organism, every inanimate object, and even in thoughts and abstract concepts.

Nature religions are founded on the belief that every living organism contains a vital force (soul) that is detachable from its body and capable of independent existence in its own right. These forces make up a suprahuman realm of reality that believers regard as being just as real as the physical world of rocks, trees, and plants. Nature religions are thus a form of animism: a belief that everything in the world, both animate and inanimate, has its own spirit.

Although the term *nature religion* is a common and useful shorthand to refer to the beliefs and practices of a number of peoples, those beliefs and practices do not constitute religions in the modern sense of the word. *Religion* is a narrowly defined word that comes from the Latin verb *religare* ("to bind"). Religion always assumes an

Below: To Native Americans of the Plains region, landscapes such as the Badlands of South Dakota, pictured here, and the nearby Black Hills were sacred places full of spiritual significance.

A Misleading Misjudgment

During the 19th and early 20th centuries, many observers dismissed nature religions as being "primitive" and thus not as worthy of attention as other belief systems. Such a view was strongly influenced by the theories of British anthropologist Edward Tylor (1832–1917), whose 1861 ethnological study *Anahuac; Mexico and the Mexicans, Ancient and Modern* established the concept of "progressive cultural evolution." Tylor argued that all societies develop in religious terms from animistic beliefs (of which nature religion is one type) toward monotheistic religions such as Christianity and Islam.

Tylor concluded that a belief in spiritual beings animating all things—from humans and animals to rivers, thunderstorms, and celestial bodies—was the earliest form of religion. Most modern scholars concur with that finding. However, he argued that fear of the power of these spiritual beings and natural forces led people to worship them. That worship, he argued, gave rise to the emergence of deities and thus evolved into a form of polytheism, or the worship of numerous gods. In turn, the pantheon of polytheistic religions was eventually supplanted by the single, all-powerful god of a monotheistic religion. Tylor's interpretation of an "evolution" of religions influenced a generation of renowned anthropologists, such as British scholars Robert R. Marett (1866–1943) and James Frazer (1854–1941), author of *The Golden Bough*.

Such evolutionary theories of religion are based on the premise that religions develop along the same lines as science and technology—since automobiles today are more advanced than they were a hundred years ago, the same must apply to belief systems. The flawed logic of this theory was highlighted by archaeological discoveries in the middle of the 20th century, including prehistoric cave paintings at Altamira in Spain and Lascaux in France. The artworks showed clearly that Paleolithic peoples, from about 30,000 BCE onward, had a highly developed sense of the possibility of communication with various environmental powers.

Today there is a general acceptance that, although nature religions predated modern religions, they did not necessarily precede them in an evolutionary sense. Nor were they less intellectually challenging than the belief systems that displaced them after the spread of literacy. The respect that nature religions showed toward the environment was the product of experience and intelligent reflection, not of unreasoning terror of the unknown, bad dreams, or simple ignorance.

Above: The Murussu Dragon, shown here on a brick from the ancient Mesopotamian city of Babylon, was the symbol of the city's high god Marduk. According to early anthropologists, the emergence of a chief god in a pantheon of deities was one step in the evolution of nature religions to monotheism.

The Green Man

Although many deities connected with the earth and fertility have been female, there have also been several notable male deities associated with these areas. One was Mars, who was originally an agricultural god responsible for protecting the crops and fields of his people. It was only later that he became the Roman god of war, assuming a more traditionally masculine role.

A popular figure from medieval European folklore, the Green Man, suggests the survival of the association between nature and the masculine. The Green Man is popularly a gigantic figure who lives in the forests and is often covered in leaves or grass. He carries a wooden staff, which sprouts shoots as a result of his fertility. The Green Man, however, represents untamed nature. For the farming peoples of Europe, he retained a certain element of threat as well as being a symbol of the richness of the natural world. He could be violent against those who were inflicting wanton damage on the environment.

The Green Man's association with nature is closely bound to the seasons and the natural cycle of growth, death, and rebirth. Traditionally he was celebrated in spring, when countries in the northern hemisphere were recovering from winter. Rebirth festivals held in May invoked the Green Man and included activities such as dancing around green trees, called maypoles, and feasting. Often during these May festivals a representation of the Green Man made from gingerbread was ritually eaten. This enabled people to absorb symbolically the figure's regenerative powers.

Right: This image of the Green Man is taken from a pamphlet of ballads printed in England in the 17th century.

underlying structure of divinely revealed rules, laws, and commandments that "bind" its believers into a coherent religious community. Many indigenous peoples, on the other hand, do not even have a word for "religion" in their language. Their closest equivalent is often a word meaning "way" or "path." In this sense, they follow the way of nature, not the religion of nature.

Historians and scientists have traditionally considered nature religions as "inferior" to either monotheistic or polytheistic religions (see box, page 954). In contrast with those religions, for example, they have no deities, prophets, saints, complex belief systems, and often no formal rituals. However, many people today find much appeal in ideas from Native American, African, and other nature religions that seem to offer a closer understanding of the value of

the earth and the environment. They believe that an increased emphasis on the spiritual value and meaning of the natural world brings humans back into contact with an age of harmony that is now lost. Elements of nature religions, such as showing respect for trees and animals, for example, often feature in the arguments of conservationists and environmental campaigners.

A living tradition

Nature religions are the earliest known form of religion. Their roots lie in the apparent spirituality of the earth, whether it be made manifest as lightning flashing across the sky or waves crashing against a cliff. Beyond such dramatic displays, ancient peoples believed that events such as a bountiful harvest or a drought were also evidence that the

Right: This bronze figure made in India around 1100 shows the Hindu god Siva in his incarnation as Nataraja, lord of the dance. Nataraja was associated with both creation and destruction. This dualistic character echoed a dualism included in many nature religions.

natural world was alive with a spiritual force. Around the world, people believed that the energies of the earth were more keenly felt in certain places, which were in turn accorded a special reverence. Many such sacred sites were distinguished by their extreme natural beauty or the strangeness of their formation. They included mountains, rivers, waterfalls, caves, and groves of trees. They continued to be revered in many societies even after more elaborate belief systems and mythologies emerged.

There is evidence that in prehistoric times nature religions were practiced by, among others, Native Americans, Balts, Celts, Greeks, and Slavs, as well as by Finno-Ugric, Italic, and Nordic-Germanic peoples. As mythologies developed, so the same impulse that lay behind nature religions was reflected in a continuing concern with the forces of nature, with the establishment of sacred places, and with the interdependence of, for example, the hunter and the hunted animal.

Virtually everywhere, nature religions have been subsumed, perhaps initially by a polytheistic mythology and later by a monotheistic religion, such as Christianity. Traditionally, commentators have seen this progression as reinforcing the idea that nature religions were somehow "primitive." However, today it is becoming more widely accepted that to imply a hierarchy of belief systems is misleading, and that many early belief systems were in fact just as theologically and intellectually rigorous and spiritually rewarding as the supposedly more "sophisticated" religions that came after them.

Although few nature religions have survived in modern societies, many of the core ideas that underlie them remain highly attractive, and throughout the world many people have adopted certain elements of traditional, earth-based beliefs. Such people are now loosely termed animists, pagans, or pantheists. Unlike ancient nature religions, however, which formed a coherent belief system and were originally practiced by nearly all the people within a certain geographical area, today's practices are personal rather than community based. Their adherents select elements from traditional beliefs on a "pick and mix" basis.

Monism

Nature religions are characterized by monism. This is different from monotheism. The god of a traditional monotheistic religion places himself above nature, even though he is regarded as its creator. Monism, on the other hand, emphasizes unity among all things. The word comes from the Greek *monos*, meaning "one," "single," or "alone."

People who have a monistic view of the world perceive the world as an organic whole, which is alive, conscious, and fluid. In this complex web, everything is interconnected. None of its parts is capable of existence when disconnected from that whole. This view forms the essence of the Gaia hypothesis, a theory developed in the 1960s by scientist James Lovelock.

Monism in this sense is an ancient idea. It occurs for example in the Vedic writings of early India, and it is linked to other belief systems that suggest the existence of one true reality. In this absolute sense of monism, the apparent differences between things—between rocks and trees, for example—are appearances only. They are illusions. Everything is an expression of the one reality.

Not all nature religions are exclusively monistic. Many are also closely linked to dualism, a theory that the world or some part of it, such as an individual human being, consists of two essentially different kinds of thing. This idea is characterized by the struggle between two opposing forces.

Dualism is an important element of many monotheistic belief systems. Islam, Christianity, and Judaism, for example, see reality as being made up of opposing factors such as

Buddhism and Nature

Although Buddhism has a founder, scriptures, and organized traditions, its views on nature mirror those of nature religions. For example, trees play an mportant part in Buddhism. In the late sixth century BCE the Buddha himself was said to have attained a state of enlightenment while sitting beneath a bodhi tree. Later stories claimed that the Buddha had been a tree-spirit in 30 of his earlier lives—29 times as a female tree-spirit and once as a king of tree-spirits.

In the Tendai sect of late-10th-century Japan, the abbot of a Buddhist monastery taught that the natural process of plant life had religious significance. A plant's sprouting showed its desire for enlightenment, its remaining in one place was its practice of discipline, its seeds showed its attainment of enlightenment, and its withering was its entry into nirvana.

In the early 12th century another Tendai scholar went further by underlining the difference between nature and the human world. He taught that the mysterious principle of Buddha-nature lives in all plants and trees as a kind of "original enlightenment" that has nothing impure in it and does not need to be sought. Just because of what they are, trees and plants intrinsically possess an underlying Buddha-nature and are already fully enlightened beings in their own right. In other words, humans must strive to attain an enlightenment that nature already has.

Below: A silk painting from Japan shows a Buddhist monk contemplating a natural scene.

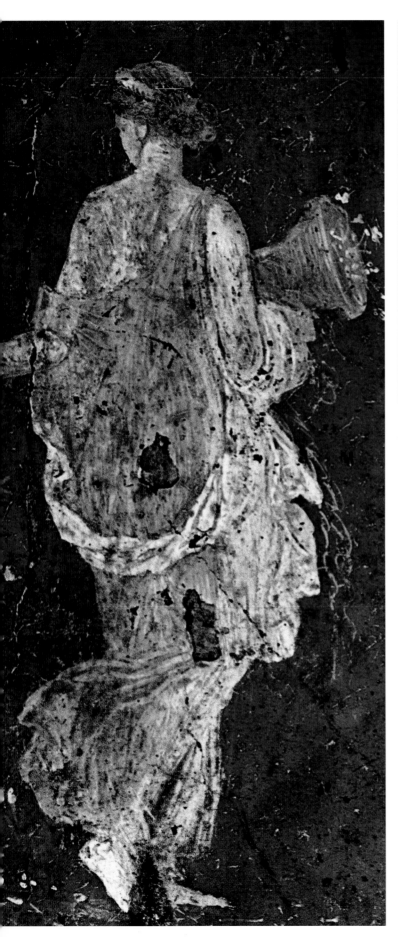

Left: Flora, shown in a first-century-CE fresco, was the Roman goddess of flowers. Many deities from classical mythologies reflected ancient origins connected to nature religions.

The End of Nature Religions?

Some people believe that the reason nature religions went into retreat was not the rise of monotheistic religions, but rather a long process of changes in the way in which humans relate to the environment, particularly those changes that opened a gap between human experience and the natural world. Such changes included, for example, the domestication of animals, the rise of urban culture, and the coming of the Industrial Revolution in the late 18th and early 19th centuries. In the late 19th century, such physical developments had an intellectual counterpart in the emergence of theories of psychology. The key to understanding the psyche is introspection, which requires a withdrawal from the natural world. Since people spend so much time thinking about thinking, critics ask, is it any wonder that they have lost the link between themselves and external reality? Modern nature religionists have regularly denounced psychoanalysis and its founders, Sigmund Freud (1856–1939) and Carl Gustav Jung (1875–1961), for "dehumanizing" nature.

good and evil, mind and body, and spirit and flesh. The idea of similar pairs of opposing forces predates monotheistic religion by thousands of years. There was a basis for them in the oppositions of nature itself: the day and the night, the barren winter and the bountiful summer, the hot fire and the cooling water. In a monotheistic approach, the opposites are engaged in a conflict that will eventually produce a winner: good will triumph over evil, the mind over the body, the spiritual over the earthly. In nature religions, on the other hand, the opposing pairs are more often perceived as being engaged in an eternal dance rather than a war. Each must depend on the other and neither could exist independently.

KATHLEEN JENKS

Bibliography

Goodenough, Ursula. *The Sacred Depths of Nature.* New York: Oxford University Press, 1998.

Gottlieb, Roger, ed. *This Sacred Earth: Religion, Nature, Environment.* New York: Routledge, 2000.

Lovelock, James. *Gaia: A New Look at Life on Earth.* New York: Oxford University Press, 2000.

SEE ALSO: Dualism; Monotheism; Native Americans; Natural Forces; Paganism; Polytheism; Prehistoric Religion; Scandinavia.

The people of ancient Egypt were almost entirely dependent on grain for food. Consequently the harvest was a sacred and very important time of year for them. After the grain had been harvested with small sickles, it was laid on a threshing floor, where it was trampled by cattle. The weight of the animals' bodies would separate the grains from the stalks. In the Nile Valley, the most fertile region of Egypt, winnowing was then carried out by picking up the grain on short-handled wooden paddles and tossing it into the air. The heavier grains would fall to earth while the lighter chaff (the stalks and husks of the cereal) would be blown away. It is thought that the scarves were intended to keep the harvesters' hair free of falling chaff.

Above: This image of a winged Nepthys was carved on the tomb of Egyptian pharaoh Ramses III (reigned 1198–1166 BCE).

In early agriculture-based cultures it was not uncommon for deities who ruled over the harvest to be linked with cycles of death and rebirth. In Greece, for example, Demeter, goddess of grain, was associated with death through her daughter Persephone, queen of the underworld. In Egypt, Nepthys, Isis, and Osiris were similarly linked with death, rebirth, harvesting, and grain.

In addition to the headdress and scarf, Nepthys wore a long, straight gown with shoulder straps. Although the dress is represented as tight and figure-hugging, archaeological

Nepthys in Drama

Three of the most important surviving documents that mention Nepthys are known collectively as "The Songs of Isis and Nepthys." These texts, all written in Egyptian, date from the fourth century BCE, although they may have been copied or translated from earlier originals.

"The Songs of Isis and Nepthys" are ritual plays based on the story of Osiris. The drama itself consists of a series of speeches by Isis and Nepthys in which the goddesses lament the death of Osiris and ask him to return to them. The most interesting parts of the texts, however, are the instructions on how the drama or rite is to be performed. Each of the works begins with detailed directions about the correct method of enacting the rite, who the actors in the drama should be, and how they should be attired. The directions state that the two goddesses are to be portrayed by priestesses wearing wigs on their shaven heads and with the names of the goddesses inscribed on their arms. It is also stipulated that the priestesses should be young and attractive. Stage directions of this type are very rare in ancient drama, and they offer a valuable clue to the way in which religious ceremonies were performed in ancient Egypt.

Left: Nepthys mourning Osiris. This painted wooden ornament dates from between about 945 and 715 BCE. Nepthys helped her sister Isis piece together the god's dismembered corpse.

remains of similar dresses worn by ancient Egyptian women suggest that most dresses were much looser. Archaeologists believe that the tighter style was originally worn by women of all classes, including royalty, but that over time it became the special garb of goddesses only. As a garment for goddesses, especially Nepthys and Isis, the dress is often decorated with geometric patterns that might be intended to represent beadwork.

Generally, the only way of distinguishing images of Nepthys from those of Isis is by the different headdresses that they wore: Isis wore a throne (instead of a palace) on top of her scarf. Sometimes the goddesses might be depicted with wings on their backs. With these, and with their arms, they were believed to embrace the souls of the dead. The basic image of Nepthys remained unchanged for thousands of years, although occasionally Isis and Nepthys were shown as kites, birds of prey of the hawk family.

Greek overlay

The story of Isis and Osiris was enduringly popular throughout the ancient Egyptian civilization. It even survived into the Ptolemaic Kings Period (304–30 BCE), during which Egypt was ruled by Macedonian Greeks. These invaders established themselves from 332 BCE, the year in which Egypt was conquered by Alexander the Great (356–323 BCE), founder of the city of Alexandria. Ptolemaic kings were descendants of Ptolemy I (ruled 323–285 BCE), who had been a general in Alexander's army. During the Ptolemaic Kings Period, Greek became the language used most often by Egypt's ruling classes. Although ancient Egyptian gods continued to be worshiped, many of them became known by Greek versions of their names and assumed some of the characteristics and myths of their Greek namesakes. Temple inscriptions were still written in hieroglyphs, but hymns and prayers to the gods were inscribed in other forms of the ancient Egyptian language or in Greek.

LYN GREEN

Bibliography

Cotterell, Arthur. *Oxford Dictionary of World Mythology.* Oxford: Oxford University Press, 1986.

Redford, Donald B. *The Oxford Essential Guide to Egyptian Mythology.* New York: Oxford University Press, 2003.

Shaw, Ian, ed. *The Oxford History of Ancient Egypt.* New York: Oxford University Press, 2000.

Wilkinson, Richard H. *The Complete Gods and Goddesses of Ancient Egypt.* New York: Thames and Hudson, 2003.

SEE ALSO: Demeter; Egypt; Geb; Isis; Nut; Osiris; Persephone; Seth.

NEPTUNE

In Roman mythology, Neptune was the god of the sea. He was the son of Saturn and Ops; his brother was Jupiter. He was the husband of Amphitrite, and the father of Triton.

The Roman god Neptune became, through identification with the Greek Poseidon, the divine lord of the sea. This equivalence was established as early as the fourth century BCE, when Neptune first appeared on coins holding a trident (a long, three-pronged, pitchfork-shaped fish harpoon), which had been the main symbol of the Greek god. Neptune, like Poseidon, was conventionally represented as a naked, bearded figure in the prime of his maturity, very much like his divine brother Jupiter. He lived in a golden house deep beneath the sea. His chariot glided across the waters so quickly that the axles of its wheels never got wet.

In Greek mythology, Poseidon's wife was the beautiful nymph Amphitrite, and in Rome Neptune was celebrated as being betrothed to the same goddess. Neptune, like Poseidon, was one of the few gods to whom bulls were sacrificed, and the Roman god also adopted his Greek predecessor's special affinity for horses. One major characteristic of Poseidon was his role as the Earth Shaker,

Below: This painting by Peter Paul Rubens (1577–1640) of Neptune calming the storm is based on an episode from Virgil's Aeneid.

who caused seismic tremors. This attribute did not become part of Neptune's usual functions. Indeed, while the Greek Poseidon was in many respects the embodiment of the elemental, irrational forces of nature, Neptune was usually depicted by the Romans as a friendly and helpful god. At one point in the *Aeneid* by Virgil (70–19 BCE), a prophecy made by the oracle of Apollo on Delos teaches the Trojan hero Aeneas that he must seek out a place to settle. Aeneas's perilous journey to Italy to found Lavinium is eased by Neptune's intervention. Fearful of a new Troy being founded in Italy, the Roman goddess Juno—who took the side of the Greeks in the war against the Trojans—orders a storm to disrupt Aeneas's journey. Neptune stills the storm and calms the sea to ensure the safe passage of Aeneas, the ancestor of the Roman people.

Although by the dawn of the Common Era Neptune had taken on nearly all the characteristics and responsibilities of Poseidon, the Roman god's true origins were almost certainly not Greek. His Latin name has a possible counterpart in the Etruscan divinity Nethuns. This god might be the forerunner of Neptune, but there are problems with such an interpretation. While Neptune was one of the most ancient Roman gods—a note of his festival, the Neptunalia, celebrated on July 23, appears in the oldest pre-Julian calendar—the name of Nethuns did not feature in any pre-Roman Etruscan religious (liturgical) documents. It is thus generally assumed that the Etruscans at some point adopted the Roman Neptune into their pantheon, rather than vice versa.

Although there is no firm evidence, there are strong indications that the Romans derived the god Neptune from their Indo-European heritage (the Etruscan language was not Indo-European in origin). In Old Irish, which is an Indo-European language, there was a water divinity known as Nechtan, a name that can be traced to a common root with the Latin Neptunus. Old Welsh (which is closely related to Irish) has a rare counterpart Neithon, and this too may be related to

Right: This statue of Neptune adorns the Trevi Fountain in Rome, Italy, celebrating the god's association with fresh water.

Neptunus. Irish lore tells of Nechtan's Hill (located in modern County Kildare, Ireland), which had a sacred and secret well. The light of knowledge was said to reside in this well, to which a formidable taboo was attached: only the water god Nechtan and his three cupbearers were permitted to approach its source of water. However, Nechtan's wife, Boand, broke the ban. Either to purify herself of guilt or perhaps out of defiance and daring, Boand approached her husband's well. When she did, the waters burst forth violently and pursued her as she fled in terror toward the sea, creating a great river, the Boyne

Left: The planet Neptune was named for its blue, watery appearance.

Rome near the banks of the Tiber River. It was probably nearby that the celebrations took place. Historian Dio Cassius (c. 150–c. 235 CE) adds the information that Agrippa, an associate and friend of Emperor Augustus, completed a building named the Basilica of Neptune, also on the Campus Martius. It therefore seems likely that Neptune enjoyed a special place with the god Mars in the religious ideology of the Campus Martius, which was in many ways the most popular quarter of ancient Rome. Neptune and Mars both appear on a large marble frieze of the early first century BCE that was unearthed on the Campus Martius, probably on the site of Neptune's temple. The frieze, which likely adorned the base of a large statue podium, shows the wedding of Neptune and Amphitrite (or Salacia) accompanied by a cortege of water nymphs and sea creatures. Pliny, in the passage mentioned above, seems to describe this very monument. At a slightly later date a separate relief was added to the monument depicting a ritual sacrifice to Mars, who is shown by his altar at the conclusion of a census. The pairing of Mars, the god of war, and Neptune, who by Augustan times was envisioned as the god of the sea, was almost certainly prompted by Roman land and naval victories. Yet Neptune's old Roman

(named for Boand), in her wake.

It is significant that Nechtan, while a god of waters, was not a god of the sea. He has special associations with a particular sacred well. Linguists usually relate the Latin Neptunus and its cognates in Old Irish to a root meaning "wetness, dampness, moisture." The Roman Neptune was almost certainly not, in origin, a sea deity but a god of freshwater sources who protected wells and rivers. While in the most common Roman version of Greek myth, Neptune's wife was, like Poseidon's, Amphitrite, Latin authors also recalled that Neptune had a cult partner, later interpreted as his wife, named Salacia. Her name has usually been related to a root meaning "spring," both in the sense of "water" and in the sense of "jump." Salacia, then, seems to personify the springing forth of waters, an activity that lay within Neptune's area of responsibility.

The festival of Neptune

Neptune's great festival, the Neptunalia, makes evident the god's role in bringing forth water. The feast was held annually on July 23, a time of year when scorching heat and the danger of drought made the need for water critical. Neptune's presence was felt to be embodied in the water of the river, and the people must have invoked the god for continuing help at such a crucial time. According to Pliny the Elder (23–79 CE) in *Natural History*, Neptune had a shrine (later a temple) in the Circus Flaminius, the large open space on the Campus Martius (the Field of Mars) in

Neptune in Art

Neptune is one of the Roman deities most frequently depicted in art. Among the most famous paintings of the sea god are two works of the 17th century. One is *The Triumph of Neptune and Amphitrite*, painted about 1610 by French artist Nicolas Poussin (1594–1665). The other, based on Virgil's description in the *Aeneid*, is *Neptune Calming the Tempest* (1635) by Flemish artist Peter Paul Rubens (1577–1640) (see page 965). The former is housed in the Philadelphia Museum of Art; the latter belongs to Harvard University.

Of the countless statues of Neptune himself, either alone or with his horses and attendant minor sea deities, perhaps the most celebrated is the work by Michelangelo's apprentice Bartolommeo Ammannati (1511–1592), which stands in the Piazza della Signoria in the heart of Florence, Italy.

Above: Built around 460 BCE, the Temple of Neptune is one of the great surviving classical buildings in Paestum, Italy.

festival, the Neptunalia, originally had nothing to do with war or with military victory: it was a celebration and an invocation of springwater.

Few details have survived about what went on at the festival. We do know that leafy arbors or booths (*tabernaculum*) were constructed from the boughs of trees to shade the worshipers from the summer sun. The ordinary folk seem to have camped out along the banks of the Tiber. There was surely a holiday atmosphere in the celebration of the Neptunalia, much as there was in the New Year's feast of Anna Perenna on March 15, when the Romans also set up rude huts of branches and boughs on the same Campus Martius. On that day they drank wine and sang and danced in happy fellowship, wishing each other well for the year ahead. Such a spirit of camaraderie also marked the Neptunalia. The poet Horace (65–8 BCE) seemed to recall this holiday mood in his *Odes*, where he pondered how best to celebrate Neptune's festival day. He writes that he will open a jar of choice wine reserved for a special occasion and will sing into the night, exchanging alternate verses with his beloved Lyde, praising Neptune and his sea goddesses.

The festivities were later enhanced in Roman imperial times by the addition of games (Ludi Neptunales), which included chariot and boat races and other naval spectacles. The appeal to ordinary folk of a midsummer celebration is clear from the fact that the Neptunalia are mentioned in "rustic calendars," the ancient lists of festivals observed by country dwellers. Roman poet Ausonius (c. 310–c. 395 CE) gave a vivid account of the Neptunalia in the fourth century, attesting to the enduring popularity of the festival, which enjoyed a much longer life than most other pre-Christian Roman holidays. Over time, as Roman influence spread, Neptune was identified with a host of water divinities. In Rome, however, the character of the old Neptune persisted, especially in the celebration of his summer festival, into the late imperial epoch, c. 310 CE.

DANIEL P. HARMON

Bibliography

Horace, and David West, trans. *The Complete Odes and Epodes.* New York: Oxford University Press, 2000.

Virgil, and Robert Fitzgerald, trans. *The Aeneid.* New York: Vintage, 1990.

SEE ALSO: Aeneas; Apollo; Ireland; Juno; Mars; Nymphs; Poseidon; Saturn; Triton; Zeus.

NEREUS

Nereus, whose name in Greek means "wet one," was a sea god associated with the Mediterranean Sea in general and the Aegean Sea in particular. He was regarded as a wise old man who had the ability to see the future as well as to change into a variety of different shapes at will.

advice on how to steal the golden apples from the Garden of the Hesperides. Nereus, reluctant to answer Heracles, changed into many different shapes in an effort to escape from him. However, Heracles eventually grabbed hold of the sea god and refused to let go of him until he got his prophecy. This story has strong parallels with myths involving Proteus, another sea god, prophet, and shape-changer. Greek king Menelaus grappled with Proteus—who tried to evade capture by changing himself into, among other things, a lion, a snake, a tree, and running water—in order to learn how he could get home to Greece after the Trojan War. The similarities between the

Nereus was the son of Gaia, the earth goddess, and Pontus, the personification of the sea. His family tree demonstrated the inbreeding that was common in the Greek pantheon. His mother was also his grandmother, having given birth to Pontus through a union with the sky god Aether. Further, Doris, wife of Nereus, was another of Gaia's children, although her father was Oceanus, the personification of the river that the Greeks believed encircled the earth. In his epic poem *Theogony*, Greek author Hesiod (fl. 800 BCE) praised Nereus for his manner, calling him: "Trustworthy and gentle, and never forgetful of what is right." These qualities made the deity an ideal tutor for Aphrodite, the goddess of love.

Shapeshifter

The prophetic and shapeshifting abilities of Nereus were clearly demonstrated in the 11th of Heracles' 12 labors. Heracles went to ask the god's

Right: This ancient Roman sculpture portrays a Nereid—one of the 50 daughters of Nereus—riding a sea serpent.

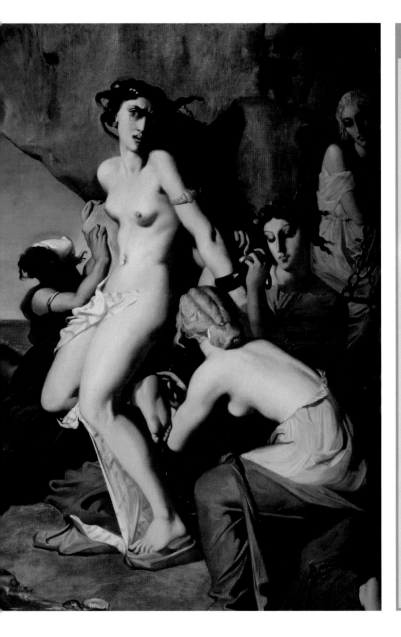

two legends are so great that some scholars have even suggested that Nereus and Proteus were one and the same—both are described by Homer, the famous Greek poet of the ninth or eighth century BCE, as "the old man of the sea." According to other sources, however, Proteus, unlike Nereus, was the son of either Poseidon or Oceanus.

Nereus and Poseidon

In the Greek pantheon, Nereus, although an ally of Poseidon, was a minor deity compared to the mighty king of the sea. *Dionysiaca*, a Greek epic poem by Nonnus (fl. c. 450–470 CE), contains an account of how Nereus helped Poseidon in a battle against Dionysus, the god of wine, after the latter had claimed the island of Naxos for himself. Historians believe that Nereus was worshiped before the arrival of Greek-speaking peoples in Greece

around 2100 BCE. Nereus was their preeminent sea god, but he was later overshadowed by a new culture and its new gods, such as Poseidon and Zeus. One piece of evidence in support of this view is that the name of Nereus's daughter, Amphitrite, is not Greek in origin. Some academics think that the *trit* part of the name represents a pre-Greek Indo-European word for "sea."

ANDREW CAMPBELL

Bibliography

Hesiod, and M. L. West, ed. *Theogony; and Works and Days.* New York: Oxford University Press, 1999.

Homer, and Robert Fagles, trans. *The Iliad and the Odyssey.* New York: Penguin Books, 1999.

SEE ALSO: Andromeda; Aphrodite; Dionysus; Gaia; Galatea; Heracles; Jason; Menelaus; Oceanus; Poseidon; Proteus; Thetis.

NESTOR

Nestor was one of the Greek rulers drawn into the Trojan War. He was known for the beauty of his voice, and his persuasive oratory was described in the epic poem the *Iliad* as "sweeter than honey," even though his tales were often long and rambling.

Above: This image of Nestor was painted on a Greek vase in the fifth century BCE.

Nestor was the youngest of the 12 sons of Neleus, king of Pylos in Greece, and Chloris. While Nestor was away from Pylos, the legendary Greek hero Heracles slaughtered Neleus and all of Nestor's brothers. Heracles had been angry at Neleus for not cleansing him of the sin of having killed Iphitus, the son of Neleus's close friend. When Nestor returned to Pylos, he ascended his father's throne.

The Trojan War

It is in the *Iliad*, the epic poem of the Trojan War by Greek poet Homer (c. ninth–eighth century BCE), that Nestor appears most often. Although Nestor was very old when the war began, he still had much to offer—his ability to fight courageously was undiminished and, with his sons Antilochus and Thrasymedes, he brought 90 ships to the Greeks' cause.

The attribute Nestor was most admired for, however, was his wisdom, which came to the Greeks' assistance at several crucial moments during the war. After the Greek hero Achilles and the Greek commander Agamemnon quarreled—the result of Agamemnon taking Achilles' concubine to be his own—Nestor attempted to mediate between the two men. He suggested that an embassy go to Achilles' tent and inform him of Agamemnon's remorse at his action and his offer of riches if Achilles rejoined the fighting. This advice was in vain, but at other times Nestor had more success, such as when he calmed the Greeks after Achilles' death. Furthermore, Nestor had the foresight to sail away from Troy sooner than most other Greeks. His sense of an impending catastrophe was well founded. In revenge for the Lesser Ajax's rape of Trojan princess

Cassandra in her sanctuary, the war goddess Athena sent a storm that destroyed much of the Greek fleet. Nestor, in contrast, returned to Pylos safely.

Legends

According to Homer, Nestor enjoyed telling long, rambling stories. He would recount how, as a young man, he fought against the centaurs, performed heroically in the Epeian War, won boxing matches and spear-throwing contests at the funeral games of Amarynceus, and nearly defeated the Moliones, twin sons of Poseidon.

As for Nestor himself, there are no tales of his death and no records of a King Nestor of Pylos ever having existed. In 1939, however, archaeologists discovered the site of a large, ancient palace near Pylos. It is referred to as the palace of Nestor.

BARBARA GARDNER

Bibliography
Homer, and Robert Fagles, trans. *The Iliad*. New York: Penguin USA, 2003.

SEE ALSO: Achilles; Agamemnon; Ajax; Demigods and Heroes; Heracles; Odysseus.

NIBELUNGS

In Germanic mythology, a Nibelung is any member of a race of people who lived principally in Burgundy (part of modern France) and also in the Rhineland (part of modern Germany).

Although there are many myths about the Nibelungs, the most famous medieval account is found in the *Nibelungenlied* ("Song of the Nibelungs"), a long poem by an unknown author, probably written in Austria about 1200 CE. In the 19th century, the story was adapted by German composer Richard Wagner (1813–1883) to form the basis of *Der Ring des Nibelungen*, a cycle of four operas—*Das Rheingold* ("Rhinegold"), *Die Walküre* ("The Valkyries"), *Siegfried*, and *Götterdämmerung* ("Twilight of the Gods").

The outline of the most important Nibelung story is as follows. Siegfried, an ambitious prince, travels incognito from his native Holland to the city of Worms in the hope of wooing Kriemhild, a Nibelung princess. Soon after he arrives there, he is recognized by Hagen, who tells his liege lord—Kriemhild's brother, King Gunther—about Siegfried's heroic past. Many of Siegfried's previous exploits are adaptations of stories originally about Sigurd, one of the great heroes of Scandinavian mythology. These legends include his acquisition of an unspecified treasure: in some versions it was a mass of precious metals and jewels, and a cloak of invisibility; in others it was a solitary magical gold ring (see box, page 974).

Saved by Siegfried

When the Danes and Saxons declare war, Siegfried offers to lead the Nibelungs and distinguishes himself in battle. On his return he meets Kriemhild for the first time, and they fall in love. Then Gunther becomes fascinated with Brunhild, a queen who says she will marry only a king who can match her own extraordinary powers. The character of Brunhild, too, is derived from earlier Scandinavian legend: in Old Norse myths she is Brynhild,

a Valkyrie, one of the beautiful maidens who serve Odin and ride over the battlefields to claim dead heroes and take them to Valhalla.

Gunther asks Siegfried to help him to win Brunhild, and promises him his sister's hand in marriage if he succeeds. They go together to Brunhild's palace, where Siegfried pretends to be Gunther's vassal, or servant. In the ensuing series of contests and trials of strength, Gunther appears to match Brunhild, but it is all an illusion: the king merely goes through the motions while the feats are performed by Siegfried beside him hidden by a cloak of invisibility.

Brunhild accepts that she has met her match, and marries Gunther. Gunther keeps his promise to Siegfried, who duly marries Kriemhild. Yet it is not long before Brunhild grows suspicious of her husband. When she ridicules Kriemhild for marrying a vassal, Kriemhild angrily reveals the deception that brought Brunhild and Gunther together.

When Brunhild realizes that she has been duped, she devotes all her energies to taking revenge on the Nibelungs. The problem, of course, is that Siegfried has already shown that he is her equal in power. However, she enlists the support of Hagen, who wheedles his way into Kriemhild's confidence and learns from her Siegfried's fatal flaw—a weak spot between the shoulder blades. Hagen takes advantage of this information, stabbing Siegfried to death during a hunting expedition while the hero is stooping to drink from a brook.

The vengeance of Kriemhild

After Siegfried's death, Brunhild disappears from the story. Kriemhild is devastated by the death of her husband. She blames Gunther, and for years the two siblings are estranged. Eventually, they reconcile in order to make use of Siegfried's treasure, which is brought to Worms. Hagen fears the renewed influence of the princess, so he throws the treasure into the Rhine River.

Etzel, the king of the Huns, then comes to Worms. When he asks for Kriemhild's hand, she accepts, seeing

Right: In this illustration by Arthur Rackham (1867–1939), Alberich (see box, page 974) makes his son Hagen swear revenge on Siegfried.

Above: Ehrenfels Castle overlooks the Rhine River into which Hagen threw the treasure of the Nibelungs.

Other Versions of the Ring

In some versions of the story, Nibelung I was an early Germanic king, whose realm was named Nibelungland and whose subjects were the Nibelungs. His treasure was guarded either by a dragon or by a bad-tempered dwarf named Alberich, who was also in charge of bringing up Siegfried. Eventually the young hero grew tired of his mentor's constant insults and killed him. Siegfried then took possession of the royal treasure, which may have been extensive but may also have been simply a gold ring of power. Rings appear frequently in Norse myth—most notably Draupnir, the ring of Odin. Rings bound the chief with his men, and signified the ordered community of men and gods. The ring of the Nibelungs was the cause of Siegfried's destruction, since Hagen killed him for it. "The Song of the Nibelungs" is the account of this treachery and of the ultimate ruin of the House of Nibelung.

In other versions, Alberich was also the guardian of Tarnkappe, a cloak that rendered the wearer invisible. On the death of the dwarf, Siegfried took Tarnkappe with the rest of the treasure. In another account, after the death of Nibelung I, Alberich served the king's sons, who ruled jointly as Schilbung and Nibelung II until Siegfried killed them both in battle.

In yet another account, Siegfried does not kill Alberich: indeed, the dwarf survives the prince. After his death, Alberich gives the treasure to Siegfried's widow, Kriemhild, whom he now regards as its rightful owner. However, not long after Kriemhild gains the treasure, Hagen steals it from her and hurls it into the Rhine River.

the marriage as an opportunity to harm the Nibelungs and her brother—she is still consumed with grief and bitter at the death of Siegfried. Years later, Kriemhild persuades Etzel to invite Hagen to court. Carnage ensues. Kriemhild has Gunther killed, then captures Hagen. When Hagen refuses to reveal the whereabouts of the treasure, Kriemhild kills him with Siegfried's sword, even though he is tied up and defenseless. Kriemhild is in turn killed by Hildebrand, a knight who is outraged by her atrocities. Part of the legend of the Nibelungs is based on a historical event, the destruction of the Burgundian capital Gundahar by Attila the Hun in 437 CE.

The Volsungs

In Wagner's version of the story, Siegfried was the last of the Volsungs, a legendary dynasty founded by Odin. Odin's grandson Volsung, from whom the family took its name, was a powerful and wealthy king who had nine sons and one daughter. He thrust a sword through an oak that grew in his great hall, declaring that the weapon would belong to the hero who could pull it out. His youngest son, Sigmund, was able to do so but, according to one version of the legend, Siggeir, king of the Goths, who had married Volsung's daughter Signy or Sieglinde, coveted the sword, and treacherously killed Volsung and all the brothers except Sigmund. Siegfried was Sigmund's son. Versions of this legend are found in the Icelandic *Poetic Edda* and in the Scandinavian *Völsunga Saga*.

BARBARA GARDNER

Bibliography

Lindow, John. *Norse Mythology: A Guide to the Gods, Heroes, Rituals, and Beliefs.* New York: Oxford University Press, 2002.

Wagner, Richard, and Andrew Porter, trans. *Ring of the Nibelung.* New York: W. W. Norton, 1983.

SEE ALSO: Germanic Peoples; Odin; Scandinavia; Sigurd; Valkyries.

NIKE

Nike was the Greek goddess of victory. She was more a personification of victory than an actual character and consequently did not appear in stories. However, her symbolic importance to the Greeks in connection with battles, athletic contests, and even weddings was considerable. Many surviving representations in stone and pottery depict her dancing, running, or flying.

While one source suggested that Nike was the daughter of Polemos, the personification of war, and another related that she was the child of Zeus, king of the gods, the best-known account of her origins was provided by Greek poet Hesiod (fl. 800 BCE). He wrote in *Theogony* that Nike's mother was the underworld Styx River and that her father was the Titan Pallas. Nike's siblings, in this account, were Zelus (Aspiration), Bia (Force), and Cratos (Power). Hesiod recounted that Styx and her children were the first to join Zeus in the war against the Titans that established the sovereignty of the Olympian gods. Zelus appeared solely in connection with this myth; Cratos and Bia, however, played roles in other stories carrying out the will of Zeus. They appear, for example, in the tragedy *Prometheus Bound* by Greek dramatist Aeschylus (525–456 BCE).

Link with Athena
Nike was associated with Zeus and with his daughter Athena, goddess of arts and war. Indeed, the two female deities were sometimes combined into a single figure: Athena Nike. Phidias (fl. c. 490–430 BCE) erected a great statue of Athena inside her chief temple, the Parthenon, built on the Acropolis in Athens between 447 and 432 BCE. The sculptor included a little winged Nike fluttering in the palm of Athena's hand. Several decades after the completion of the Parthenon, the Athenians constructed a small temple of Athena Nike on a bastion above the entrance to the Acropolis. Around the temple ran a balustrade decorated with little Nikai (the plural of *Nike*) engaged in preparations for a sacrifice. Athena appears several times among them.

Below: This relief sculpture of Nike has been reconstructed from an ancient tablet unearthed at Ephesus, Turkey.

Nike and Weddings

Nike's symbolic importance extended to weddings. Her role in such ceremonies is suggested in *The Birds* by Greek comic dramatist Aristophanes. In this play, the chorus sings to the bridegroom "Hail to the victor." In addition, in ancient Greek art Nike appears in representations of the wedding cortege, flying over the cart transporting the happy couple. The linking of Nike with marriage explains the goddess's association with Eros, the god of love. In other artistic representations, Nike and Eros appear as a pair of small winged figures.

However, while Nike played a role in Greek weddings, it is not clear exactly whose victory the ceremonies were supposed to represent. While Aristophanes implies that the groom is triumphant over the bride, Nike was a familiar figure on Greek women's possessions, such as jewelry and ornamental seals, which represented power. Marriage was an indirect means for Greek women to achieve power, so it is possible that, in that sense, the bride was the victor. However, perhaps the most convincing answer is that the wedding was the joint victory of the couple. Victory, for the Greeks, was a moment when humans achieved perfection. Athletic victory was one such moment; so too was marriage, the joyous and triumphant union of two people, whether for love or personal advancement.

Nike and military victory

For the Greeks, Nike was a symbol of military victory. They prayed to the goddess for success in battles—if victory was forthcoming, they regarded it as indication of her favor. On the temple of Athena Nike, some of the Nikai are depicted building trophies of the kind Greek armies customarily left on the battlefield as tokens of their victory. These were cairns, or mounds, constructed of broken weapons and armor gathered from the fallen enemy. Such ritual objects were the concrete embodiments of Nike's favor for the winning side. No victorious Greek army would have left the battlefield without building such a trophy. They were also put up on nearby shores after sea battles.

The ancient Greeks' greatest military triumph was the naval victory over the Persians at the Battle of Salamis in 480 BCE. Writing about the battle, Greek historian Herodotus (c. 484–425 BCE) related how the Greeks remembered an oracle which promised them that "the day of freedom" would be granted by "Zeus and Lady Nike." To give thanks for the victory, the Greeks dedicated a statue to Nike at Delphi.

Besides wars and battles, Nike was important on other occasions when people sought victory, including lawsuits

Below: The Temple of Athena Nike forms part of the Acropolis that overlooks Athens, Greece.

and athletic and musical competitions. Several works by Greek dramatist Euripides (c. 486–c. 406 BCE) end with a prayer by the chorus for Nike to attend to them through life and continue to crown them—in other words, to ensure their success.

Understanding personification

Like other figures in the Greek pantheon, such as Mnemosyne (Memory), Thanatos (Death), and Polemos (War), Nike was a personification of an abstract force and not a developed personality in the manner of deities such as Zeus and Athena. However, the distinction between person and personification was not always clear. For example, at certain moments Polemos seemed to be a minor divinity in his own right and appeared as a character in a play by Aristophanes (c. 450–c. 388 BCE).

Right: The Winged Victory of Samothrace *was created in the early second century BCE. It is now housed in the Louvre in Paris, France.*

Personifications tended to develop into personalities as stories were told about them, whereupon they became objects of cult worship and were represented in art. Nike did not appear in any stories and was not the object of cult worship—the Greeks prayed for victory and offered battlefield trophies to her if they were successful, but these were tributes to a symbol rather than a person.

Yet Nike did become something of a personality through artistic representation. Greek artists frequently represented her in paintings on pottery, in small bronze figures, in stone sculptures and terra-cottas, and on jewelry, coins, and seal rings. The goddess was nearly always shown with wings, dressed in flowing garments, and in motion.

On early pottery paintings she is depicted running; in later representations she is often swooping down to touch the earth. One of the greatest sculptures of the deity, Nike of Paionios (c. 420 BCE), stood high on a pillar at the sanctuary of Olympia on the Peloponnese peninsula, supported by her bare toes which just grazed the base. In other representations, such as those on Sicilian coins that commemorated racing victories at the Olympic Games, Nike flies over chariots with her wings outspread. Another portrayal of the goddess is the eight-foot- (2.4 m-) high *Winged Victory of Samothrace* (c. 190 BCE), which shows Nike touching down on the prow of a ship. The statue, which now stands in the Louvre, in Paris, France, commemorated victory in a sea battle. Nike's Roman counterpart, the goddess Victoria, was also frequently represented by artists and sculptors. Roman Emperor Augustus (63 BCE–14 CE) placed Victoria's most important altar in the Senate House in Rome in 29 BCE.

In the world of commerce, in 1972 the name Nike was adopted by a U.S. company that has since become one of the world's leading manufacturers of sportswear and sports equipment.

JAMES M. REDFIELD

Bibliography

Bulfinch, Thomas. *Bulfinch's Mythology.* New York: Modern Library, 1998.

Hesiod, and M. L. West, trans. *Theogony; and Works and Days.* New York: Oxford University Press, 1999.

SEE ALSO: Athena; Eros; Mnemosyne; Titans; Zeus.

NILE

The Nile River flows north through Egypt and divides the country in two. The fertile land along its banks made human settlement possible in a part of North Africa that is mainly desert. Hecataeus, a Greek writer of the sixth or fifth century BCE, in a quotation usually attributed to Herodotus (c. 484–425 BCE), observed: "Egypt is the gift of the Nile."

To the ancient inhabitants of Egypt, who lived in isolated villages along its banks, the Nile River was simply *iterwu*, the river. To the Greeks it became *Neîlos*, the source of the English name Nile. It provided vital water for drinking and bathing, and the means of transportation and communication that allowed Egypt to grow into one of the greatest cultures in history. Most important of all, regular flooding made its valley fertile enough to support agriculture. The Nile took on a profound mystical significance, one that helped to confirm the Egyptians' view of their place in the universe.

The river

At 4,160 miles (6,695 km), the Nile is the longest river in the world. It rises in the mountains of eastern Africa as two separate branches: the Blue Nile from Ethiopia and the White Nile from Uganda. They join at Khartoum, Sudan, and flow north as one mighty river, eventually reaching Egypt and continuing through the country to the huge fanlike delta. There the Nile forks into two main branches, the Rosetta and the Damietta, and empties into the Mediterranean Sea. Over the centuries the course of the Nile has shifted and the nature and size of the delta and its many river branches have changed, sometimes dramatically. Each year, torrential rain in the upper reaches of the river causes its waters to swell and flood. This flooding carries with it tons of rich, fertile silt from the uplands that lie far to the south of Egypt. When the floodwaters recede, the silt is left behind.

Today, the extent of this process has been reduced by dams that have been built to control the floods. The largest and most important of these is the High Dam at Aswan, near Egypt's southern border, which was completed in 1971. However, in ancient times, from June or July to September or October, the Nile swelled and flooded along the length of the valley and throughout the delta. Silt was deposited along the Nile floodplain, forming vast tracts of fertile topsoil. The result was that Egypt, with an economy

Left: This satellite photograph of Egypt shows clearly the arid, desertified expanse of North Africa split by the fertile green strip of land along the banks of the Nile River. As one of the few parts of Egypt in which farming was possible, the area became a major human settlement.

based on agriculture, was self-supporting and prosperous. In the ancient Egyptian worldview, the annual cycle of inundation followed by crop sowing and rich harvests was evidence that the gods favored Egyptians above all others.

Hapi: god of inundation

The ancient Egyptians based their religious references on their observations of the world around them. The sky, the sun and moon, the earth, and even the air were all seen as manifestations of particular deities. The Nile River was no exception, and a number of major and minor gods were associated with it.

Commonly referred to as "the god of the Nile," Hapi was more accurately the god who personified the annual flooding. The inundation was in fact referred to as "the arrival of Hapi." The god had no major temples dedicated to him, but there is clear evidence that he was revered throughout the country for much of its history. The ancient Egyptians believed that Hapi lived in a cave at what they called "the first cataract," a waterfall near modern Aswan. There he was surrounded by crocodiles and goddesses. These goddesses were either frogs or women with the heads of frogs. Each year, at the start of the inundation, the people made sacrifices to Hapi near the first cataract, at a place named Gebel el-Silsila. One source says that a single sacrifice consisted of almost 1,100 goats.

Above: The Nile River at Luxor. The modern city is the site of Thebes, the ancient capital of Egypt.

The Nile and Cosmic Order

At the heart of Egyptian society was the principle of *maat*. This was a kind of harmony, a balance of everything in the cosmos. *Maat* symbolized an absence of chaos. It was represented by the goddess Maat, who was shown holding a feather. In the Books of the Dead, one of the illustrations showed the weighing of the heart. The dead person's heart was placed in one pan of a set of scales; the other pan held a feather or occasionally a seated or kneeling goddess Maat holding a feather. To be admitted to the afterlife, the heart could not be heavier than the feather, which represented truth and goodness. If the heart was heavier, it was a sign that it was sinful and the deceased unworthy of a life with the gods.

The reigning pharaoh was humankind's link with the gods, and his primary duty was to ensure the continuation of *maat*. If he was successful, the gods showed their approval, primarily by the annual inundation of the Nile. If the pharaoh failed and displeased the gods, then the Nile would not overflow its banks and fertilize the land. The results could be catastrophic. Drought, famine, and disease were taken as signs that the cosmic order had been disturbed.

Measuring the Nile

One of the duties of the temple priests in ancient Egypt was to measure and record the level of the rising Nile. Temple ruins still contain examples of Nilometers. This is the word used by Egyptologists for the flights of steps from the temple to the river, with marks at varying heights on the surrounding walls to gauge the rising water level. Appropriately high levels meant increased farmland and rich harvests. Excessively high levels indicated flooding that could be destructive; low levels could mean starvation. Many scholars believe that annual taxes were set according to predictions drawn from the priests' observations at the Nilometers.

These ancient gauges can be seen at the temples of Dendera, Idfu, Esna, and Philae. The island of Elephantine, at Aswan, also has a Nilometer.

Records of inundation levels were important enough to be kept. One such record is engraved on the Palermo Stone, a large stone stela, or tablet, of the Fifth Dynasty (c. 2450–c. 2325 BCE). It contained the most important events in the reign of each king to that time, including the annual flood level.n

Below: A Nilometer at Dendera, Egypt. When the river floods, the pool fills, and the depth of water can be measured.

Physically, Hapi was depicted as a man with drooping female breasts and a distended abdomen. He wore a long wig and had papyrus plants on top of his head. He also had a long, narrow, braided beard. His skin was usually, but not always, blue; his beard could be blue or green. Sometimes he carried a tray laden with produce. The physical characteristics, colors, and use of Nile plants and vegetation all contribute to an image of the fertility brought by the river's inundation.

Hapi was sometimes shown as a double image, with the two figures facing each other. One image had plants symbolizing Lower Egypt—the region of the Nile delta—the other depicted plants of Upper Egypt, the Nile valley from south of the delta to the first cataract. The figures bound the plants together. This well-known motif was known as *sma-tawy*, or "union of the two lands." Its use dates from the Old Kingdom (c. 2575–c. 2130 BCE)—Upper and Lower Egypt had been unified about 2900 BCE—but the inclusion of figures of Hapi is rather later, appearing to date from between 1292 and 1190 BCE.

Khmun and Sobek

There are numerous waterfalls or cataracts along the Nile River. To ancient Egyptians, the area of the first cataract was sacred. The first cataract is the southernmost cataract and is located near the modern city of Aswan. It was where Hapi resided and where the all-important inundation began. The ram-headed god Khmun was the guardian of the region, and he was helped by the goddesses Anukis and Satis. Together these three divinities formed a triad, or three-part family unit, with Satis being considered the wife of Khmun and Anukis their daughter.

Khmun is primarily known as a creator god who fashioned all beings—divine, human, and animal—on his potter's wheel. He was also "lord of the cataract," in which role he controlled the yearly inundation. His worship goes back at least to the earliest dynasties, and he had a center of worship on the island of Elephantine in the middle of the river at Aswan. A number of highly decorated rams have been found in ritual burials there. A long inscription on a rock on Seheil Island, slightly upstream from Aswan, pleads with Khmun to reverse seven years of famine caused by low flood levels. The inscription itself was carved during the time of the Ptolemaic Kings (304–30 BCE), but is supposed to be a copy of one from the reign of Djoser, who ruled during the 27th century BCE.

In the mythology of the Nile River there are numerous references to its greatest animal, the crocodile. Hapi's male courtiers are crocodiles, and Khmun's title, "lord of the

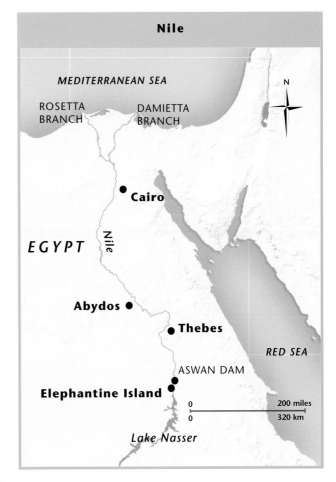

crocodiles," linked him to the crocodile god Sobek. At Khmun's temple at Esna, Sobek's mother Neith was also honored. According to one legend, the Nile River itself sprang from Sobek's sweat. In the Pyramid Texts (from about 2400 BCE), Sobek is said to have been responsible for the lush green growth along the banks of the river.

Under the Ptolemaic Kings, a whole town and priesthood were devoted to Sobek at Crocodilopolis in the northern region. Sobek, his wife Hathor, and his son Khonsu shared the Temple of Kom Ombo with the god Haroeris, also known as Horus the Elder. The small shrine to Hathor there is full of mummified crocodiles.

Osiris: god of inundation and fertility

Another god who had strong associations with the Nile River was Osiris. He was not only one of the most powerful deities, but also one of the oldest. He was also mentioned in the Pyramid Texts. Osiris is commonly thought to have been ruler of the underworld and associated with death, resurrection, and eternal life. However, this view reflects the way in which his character evolved over centuries. In the earliest times, Osiris was linked primarily with the floods and fertility.

Above: This bas-relief dating from between about 1300 and 1100 BCE shows the Egyptian crocodile god Sobek.

Osiris was often depicted with black or dark green skin, and many historians believe that this was in imitation of the rich soil left along the banks of the Nile after the waters receded.

Center of worship

Osiris was revered throughout Egypt, but the center of his worship was at Ibdju (modern Abydos). It was there that he was killed by his brother, Seth, and also there that he was buried. A great festival in honor of Osiris was celebrated at Abydos every year. Some rituals of Osiris involved grain being threshed, or beaten, into ground made fertile by flooding. It is thought that this was a way of interceding with the gods for a good harvest.

There is another link between the Nile River, fertility, and Osiris. Archaeologists have found "Osiris beds" in tombs. These are wooden frames in the shape of the god that contain Nile mud planted with grain, apparently as a symbol of resurrection or eternal life.

The Nile River itself appears frequently in stories about Osiris. In one, the jealous Seth tricked Osiris and sealed him inside an elaborate chest, which he then threw into the river. It was carried out into the Mediterranean Sea, from where it was washed up in Lebanon and became surrounded by a tree. Isis later rescued the body of her husband. In another myth, Seth found the chest and dismembered his murdered brother's body, spreading the pieces along the whole length of the Nile. Isis later found each part (all but the phallus, which Seth had fed to a crocodile) and buried it with proper funeral ceremonies. As a result, many different places along the river were able to claim that they were the burial place of Osiris.

ELIZABETH LONGLEY

Bibliography

Redford, Donald B. *The Oxford Essential Guide to Egyptian Mythology.* New York: Oxford University Press, 2003.

Wilkinson, Richard H. *The Complete Gods and Goddesses of Ancient Egypt.* New York: Thames and Hudson, 2003.

SEE ALSO: Animals; Egypt; Flood Myths; Hapi; Horus; Isis; Osiris; Seth.

NINURTA

Ninurta was the Sumero-Babylonian god of rain, thunderstorms, fertility, war, wells, canals, floods, and the south wind. His name probably meant either "Lord of the Earth" or "Lord Plow." The most important surviving myth about him recounts his battle against a monster known as Asag.

The gods of ancient Mesopotamia can often be confusing figures to study. Sometimes they were known by slightly different names in different cities. Often separate deities merged over time to become one. The surviving stories about these gods may have been passed down to us in fragments of poems from civilizations separated by thousands of years. For these reasons, the information that we have about these gods can often seem contradictory. This is certainly the case with Ninurta.

Ninurta's predecessor in the Sumerian pantheon might have been a vegetation god called Urash. However, Ninurta was also identified with Ningirsu, and the two deities are often seen as one. Ningirsu was a god of the Sumerian territory of Lagash and was worshiped there in the third millennium BCE. A local god with many responsibilities, his name meant "Lord of Girsu," a city of Lagash. As the patron deity of Lagash, he was not only a warrior and protector of the territory from invasion, but was also responsible for the fertility of the city's farmland.

Ningirsu was the son of An, the Sumerian sky god, and a locally worshiped goddess known as Gatumdug. Ninurta, however, had a different family tree. He was believed to be the son of Enlil, the earth and storm god, and Ninlil, a goddess whose name meant "Lady Air." To add to the confusion, Ninlil was sometimes known as Ninmena, and in the most important myth about Ninurta, she assumed a different name—Ninhursaga. This myth is known as the *Lugal-e*. Among the various translations of this title are "King Storm-whose-splendor-is-overwhelming" and "Oh Warrior King."

The rebellion of Asag

In the *Lugal-e* Ninurta was called on to confront a monster or demon known as Asag. Asag was made of stone and was leading the rocks of the earth in a rebellion against the gods. The rocks rolled down the mountainsides and crushed everything in their path. Ninurta launched a fearsome attack against the monster and was initially repelled. Eventually, however, Ninurta was advised by his father Enlil to use thunderstorms to defeat his foe. Ninurta followed this advice and was victorious.

After defeating the demon, Ninurta used the stones to divert mountain streams onto the plains and build a great dam to keep the Tigris River from flooding its eastern bank. In so doing, he introduced irrigation to the world. Ninlil traveled

Left: This neo-Assyrian carving from the eighth century BCE is believed to depict the god Ninurta, seen here carrying a bow.

983

to congratulate her son, and Ninurta addressed her by the name of Ninhursaga ("Lady of the Stony Desert"). Ninurta later punished the stones that had joined in the rebellion by assigning them menial tasks—he decreed that limestone should be used as the foundation for buildings, for example. In contrast he rewarded loyal stones, such as lapis lazuli, by declaring that they should be used for ornaments and decoration.

The Plowman of Enlil

The myth of Ninurta's defeat of Asag survives only in the form of fragments of poetry, and scholars argue about how the myth should be pieced together. It is also very difficult to definitively describe Ninurta's role in the Mesopotamian pantheon. Scholars generally believe that

Above: The Standard of Ur, an ornamental box made around 2650 BCE, shows scenes of agriculture, on which Ninurta gave advice, and contains lapis lazuli.

he may have been a god of fertility, although no one is absolutely sure. In Sumerian texts, he was called the "plowman of Enlil" and gave advice on farming. This side of Ninurta's character is in distinct contrast to that displayed in the *Lugal-e*, where he is depicted as a fearsome warrior. There we are given a list of creatures that Ninurta has already slain. They include a six-headed wild ram, a bison, a lion, a dragon, and a seven-headed serpent. The presence on this list of a seven-headed serpent and a lion conjures up images of the Greek hero Heracles and his 12 labors.

The warlike aspect of Ninurta's personality especially appealed to the kings who ruled the Assyrian Empire in the ninth century BCE. They worshiped Ninurta as a warrior god and chief deity, and made him patron god of their capital city, Nimrud. It was in his role as patron of the warlike rulers who would try to conquer most of ancient western Asia that Ninurta reached the height of his power and influence.

LYN GREEN

The Sisters of Ningirsu

The god Ningirsu, who was widely identified with Ninurta, had two sisters who were also important deities, Nidaba and Nanshe. Nidaba, who was sometimes called Nisaba, was the "chief scribe of heaven." Originally important in her role as patron of scribes and of motherhood, her status lessened as worship of her husband Nabu became more widespread. Nanshe, on the other hand, continued to be a very prominent goddess. King Gudea of Lagash (fl. c. 2144–2124 BCE) called on her to help Ningirsu defeat the city's enemies in battle. Nanshe also was known as the "soothsayer of the gods" and was associated with water, canals, and fisheries. Ancient Mesopotamians believed that Nanshe could give her priests the ability to interpret dreams.

Bibliography

Black, Jeremy, and Anthony Green. *Gods, Demons, and Symbols of Ancient Mesopotamia: An Illustrated Dictionary.* Austin, TX: University of Texas Press, 1992.

Roaf, Michael. *The Cultural Atlas of Mesopotamia and the Ancient Near East.* New York: Checkmark Books, 1990.

SEE ALSO: An; Enki; Enlil; Heracles; Mesopotamia.

NIOBE

The Greek queen Niobe boasted that she was more fortunate than the goddess Leto because she had more children than her. She was punished severely for this act. Niobe is a prime example of a familiar type from myth —one who destroys her own happiness by foolishly boasting of it.

N iobe was the daughter of Tantalus and the wife of Amphion, king of Thebes. Her mother was usually said to be Euryanassa, but in some accounts of her story other names are given. According to Greek poet Sappho (fl. c. 610–c. 580 BCE), Niobe was originally a companion of the goddess Leto. However, one day she made the mistake of boasting that she had more children than the goddess. This act enraged Leto to such an extent that she called on her children Artemis and Apollo to punish Niobe for her hubris.

Using the bow and arrow that were their traditional attributes, the god and goddess shot and killed all of the children of Niobe, the Niobids. As Greek writer Homer (c. ninth–eighth century BCE) says in his epic poem the *Iliad*: "Though they were only two, yet they destroyed them all." Artemis took aim at the girls while Apollo killed the boys. This is in keeping with the tradition that Artemis's arrows were a cause of death for women. Niobe's husband Amphion died immediately thereafter, either by suicide or at the hands of Apollo.

According to Homer, the gods turned all the local inhabitants to stone. So, for nine days, the children remained unburied. Finally, on the 10th day, the gods

Below: This illustration from a Greek vase depicts Niobe and was created around 460 BCE. The artist is now known as the Niobid Painter.

Above: The Massacre of Niobe's Children *by Charles Dauphin (1620–1677) depicts Apollo and Artemis slaughtering the Niobids.*

took pity and buried the children themselves. Niobe's grief was unrelenting, and she herself was eventually turned to stone. Her name became a byword for sorrow in antiquity.

Niobe in the *Iliad*

Homer's version of the story of Niobe appears toward the end of the *Iliad*. It occurs when the Greek hero Achilles is urging King Priam to break a fast caused by his grief over the death of his son Hector. Achilles invokes the story of Niobe, observing that even she stopped weeping long enough to eat. From this it is clear that from a very early date Niobe's grief was proverbial. At the same time, she was also a cautionary figure, warning people of the dangers of committing hubris by boasting of their good fortune and offending the gods.

The exact number of Niobe's children varies from source to source, but there is almost always an equal number of sons and daughters. In Homer's account, Niobe had six sons and six daughters. In a poetic version of her story by Hesiod (fl. 800 BCE), she had five of each. Elsewhere she had seven or even as many as ten of each. Various lists of names are given. For example, in *The Library*, a summary of Greek mythology attributed to the writer Apollodorus (fl. 140 BCE), the following names are

given for the male children: Sipylus, Damasichthon, Eupinytus, Ismenus, Agenor, Phaedimus, and Tantalus. The female children are listed as Ethodaia, Cleodoxa, Astyoche, Phthia, Pelopeia, Astycrateia, and Ogygia. Ovid (43 BCE–17 CE) uses most but not all of the same names for the boys, but does not name the girls. In general, such lists of names are not to be taken very seriously. The fact that many of them are also used for numerous other mythic figures suggests that they may have been made up by the writers.

In some versions of the story, two children of Niobe were said to survive. Meleboea was saved because she prayed to Leto. She was henceforth known as Chloris ("grass-green" or "pale") because she turned pale with fear and never regained her normal complexion. Together with her brother Amyklas, she built a temple to Leto. Chloris married Neleus, a son of the sea god Poseidon, and gave birth to 12 sons including Nestor, who later fought in the Trojan War. The ancient travel writer Pausanias (143–176 CE) claimed to have visited the temple that Chloris built. Pausanias also wrote that he had seen the tombs of the other children of Niobe in Thebes, and the spot on Mount Sipylon near his hometown in Asia Minor where the rock that had once been Niobe stood.

Several features of Niobe's story are echoed in other ancient Greek myths. One common theme is that of a small band of children, equally divided between boys and girls, who face some terrible danger. Some of these myths can be connected with apparently initiatory rituals in which children were secluded in temples to serve a god. For example, one legend tells of how a regular tribute of seven Athenian girls and seven boys had to be sent to the Cretan labyrinth to feed the Minotaur as compensation to King Minos for the murder of his son Androgeos. This myth was commemorated in an annual festival, the Oschophoria, in which boys paraded to the sea dressed as girls. Their mothers ran behind them offering them snacks for the long trip ahead. In Corinth, a ritual was performed in which seven girls and seven boys lived at the temple of Hera Akrai. During this period, they served the goddess as expiation for the Corinthians' murder of Medea's children in that very temple.

The myth of Niobe, with its preoccupation with the bearing of children and their subsequent death or survival and the detail of the equal number of boys and girls, suggests that she may have been connected to a similar ritual, although no evidence for one has come down to us. In any case, the myth is concerned with

Right: This marble statue, known as the Niobid of the Sallustian Gardens, was sculpted in the fifth century BCE. It shows the death of one of Niobe's daughters, killed by an arrow from Artemis.

similar issues of the survival of children and the grief of parents when they do not survive. The myth of the Niobids does not, however, contain the feature of retribution for the death of children that we find in these other examples.

Niobe in art and literature

Aeschylus (525–456 BCE) and Sophocles (c. 496–406 BCE), two of the most famous Athenian dramatists, wrote tragedies based on the myth of Niobe. However, only a few fragments of these plays survive. One of the most famous retellings of Niobe's story is found in Ovid's *Metamorphoses*. Ovid's Niobe is not merely proud of her many children, but openly contemptuous of the goddess Leto. She actively dissuades other women from worshiping at her festival. Not only is Niobe turned to stone because of her incessant mourning, but the stone weeps. Finally she is whisked away to her native country of Lycia, where the poet tells us that the mountain continues to weep still. The scene of the death of the Niobids is depicted on a famous vase by the Niobid Painter, who takes his name from this piece, while a famous sculpture of Niobe and her children existed in ancient Greece. A Roman imitation of this work is now housed in the Uffizi Gallery in Florence, Italy.

While the myth of Niobe is well known, it has produced more allusions than full-scale responses by literary artists. Shakespeare's Hamlet describes his mother at his father's funeral as "Like Niobe, all tears." Phillis Wheatley, an 18th-century African-American poet, wrote a poem inspired by both Ovid's account and a painting by Richard Wilson. Musical compositions drawing on the myth include Giovanni Pacini's opera *Niobe* (1826), and Benjamin Britten's six-part piece for oboe, "Metamorphoses after Ovid" (1951), one part of which is called "Niobe." A recent piece by American composer Stephen Scott, "The Tears of Niobe" (1990), is composed for a grand piano plucked and bowed by 10 musicians. American poet Kate Daniels's 1988 volume *The Niobe Poems* draws on the myth to deal with the theme of a contemporary mother's loss of a child.

DEBORAH LYONS

Bibliography

Homer, and Robert Fagles, trans. *The Iliad*. New York: Penguin USA, 2003.
Ovid, and A. D. Melville, trans. *Metamorphoses*. New York: Oxford University Press, 1998.

SEE ALSO: Achilles; Apollo; Artemis; Leto; Minos; Priam.

NJÖRD

Njörd was a Norse god who was associated with ships and the sea. Because seafaring played an important role in the lives of the ancient Scandinavians, Njörd was greatly revered. He was also important because he was the father of two other widely worshiped deities, Frey and Freya.

Njörd was originally a member of the Vanir. The Vanir were a group of deities who were linked to the earth, sea, lakes, and fertility; they provided a contrast to the aggressive, warlike Aesir. According to Norse mythology, the two groups of gods engaged in a great war. The two sides were evenly matched and destroyed much of each other's land. Eventually they made a truce and exchanged hostages to cement it. From among the Aesir, Hoenir and Mímir were sent to live with their

Below: This Swedish rock carving of a ship dates back to the Bronze Age, which occurred in Scandinavia between around 1500 and 500 BCE. Even as early as this, ships played an important role in daily life.

former enemies, while Njörd and his two offspring went to live with the Aesir. The trade-off was rather one-sided. While Njörd and his children were noted for their virtue, benevolence, and wisdom, Hoenir was an indecisive weakling. When the Vanir found that Hoenir was incapable of acting without his companion's advice, they cut off Mímir's head and sent it back to Odin.

Like all the Vanir, Njörd was associated with fertility and growth. However, he was also associated with a number of other phenomena as well. One saga mentions Njörd as a god of justice, along with Odin. Njörd was seen as a god of wealth, capable of granting prosperity to those who prayed to him. He was also toasted at banquets for his gift of the seasons. However, he is possibly best known as a god of the sea and the winds, making him a favorite with sailors. Fishermen venerated him for his help with the catch. Holy places associated with Njörd have been found at the heads of fjords, from where sailors and fishers set out on dangerous journeys. Propitiation of the sea god was a wise way to start a voyage.

Njörd's association with ships gave him a position of great importance in the Scandinavian world. Not only were ships a means of transportation, fishing, raids, and conquest, but they were used as funeral pyres. Set on fire and launched, they carried the bodies of dead heroes on their

Above: The Sun Chariot, discovered in Trundholm Marsh in Denmark, dates from around 1400 BCE. This intricate artifact, cast out of bronze and gold, may have been buried as a sacrifice to a predecessor of Njörd.

final journey. The beautiful god Balder, for example, was given just such a funeral after his death at the hands of Loki and Höd. His ship, carrying his armor, horse, and other necessities, was burned at sea as the other gods lamented his passing.

Like the Egyptian god Osiris, whose symbol was also a boat, Njörd and his son Frey had close ties with the underworld. Ordinary people were buried with smaller boats, or fragments of boats were placed in their graves to give their lives a heroic quality. Sometimes cremation urns were carved in the form of ships. The death ship linked Njörd and Frey to the underworld and funerary practices (see box, page 991).

The marriage between Njörd and Skadi

The main Norse myth involving Njörd revolved around his marriage to Skadi, a frost giantess. The story of how the pair came to be betrothed has its roots in a tale involving the giant Thjazi, Skadi's father. By tricking the god Loki into helping him, Thjazi managed to abduct Idun, the goddess whose golden apples ensured the gods' immortality.

preferred seaside dwellings. Njörd maintained a noisy shipyard at his home of Nóatún, and Skadi came to hate the racket. She longed to return to her quiet, snowy hills. Because Njörd wanted to stay on the seashore and Skadi wanted to live in the mountains, they came to an arrangement whereby they divided their time between the two places. However, neither could bear to live in the other's homeland. According to Icelandic writer Snorri Sturluson (1179–1241), who told the story of Njörd and Skadi in his *Prose Edda*, Njörd complained about the noise of the howling wolves in the mountains, while Skadi hated the cries of the gulls near the sea. Eventually, Skadi returned to the mountains and married Ull, god of skis. The stories told of Skadi and Njörd may connect them with rites that took place during a nine-day festival. The holiday marked the union of cold and warmth, mountains and fertile coasts.

Skadi

Skadi was associated with skiing and carried a bow and arrows. Like the Greek goddess Artemis, she was a huntress of wild animals. Some anthropologists have suggested that she may have once been seen as the consort of an obscure, pre-Viking god of skiing named Ull, since both of them were ancient deities of the north and winter. Alternatively, she originally might have been one with Ull, a masculine deity, since her name suggests a masculine form and her activities were manly ones. Her name is the same as the word for harm in Norse and is related to the Gothic word for shadow. Both of these words have a menacing quality, which may reflect the fear that the giantess inspired.

Skadi must have been an important deity, since many holy places were dedicated to her, and she was often mentioned in Norse literature. The place where she was most prominent was in the mountainous Halogaland of Norway, where the Sami or Lapps lived. The Sami were known for their skiing and archery skills, so it would be no surprise if they had a particular veneration for Skadi.

Njörd's children

Njörd was the father of two important Norse deities—the twins Frey and Freya. The identity of the children's mother is unknown, though at least one source suggests she may have been Njörd's sister, Nethus. Frey, like his father, was

Without Idun's apples, the gods began to grow old, so they devised a plan to bring her back. Loki transformed himself into a falcon and turned Idun into a nut, taking her back to Asgard in his claws. Assuming the shape of an eagle, Thjazi pursued them. However, the Aesir had built a huge fire on the walls of Asgard. Loki flew straight at it, but swerved at the last second. The less nimble Thjazi, however, was unable to avoid it and was killed.

Soon afterward, Skadi arrived at Asgard seeking revenge. To placate her, the gods said that she could take one of them as a husband as compensation, but they imposed a strange restriction on her choice. Although Skadi was free to pick any of the gods, she had to do so purely by looking at their feet. Skadi chose the god with the most beautiful feet, believing it to be the handsome god of light, Balder. The feet actually belonged to Njörd.

Njörd and Skadi's marriage was doomed. Skadi was a restless wife who could find no peace near her husband's a benevolent god who was associated with fertility. As the son of Njörd he belonged to the Vanir, but he lived with the Aesir. Historians believe that Frey was widely worshiped in Scandinavia.

Like Njörd, Frey was associated with ships. He had a ship called Skídbladnir, which was large enough to carry all the gods. It could magically be folded up small enough to

The Link between Boats and Death

Boats and death were associated in many cultures that had ties to rivers and the sea. The ancient Greeks believed that Hades, the realm of the dead, lay across the Styx River. In order to reach the underworld, the souls of the dead would have to pay the ferryman Charon to take them across. For this reason the dead were usually buried with a coin in their mouth—the coin allowed them to pay Charon for his troubles. In ancient Egypt, a death boat carried pharaohs and their retinues grandly into the next world; and the Egyptian god of death, Osiris, was often symbolized by a boat.

Above: The 70 foot (21 m) Oseberg ship, built in the ninth century CE, was constructed specifically for a funeral ceremony.

fit in a purse. Since Njörd was lord of the winds, his son's ship always moved in whatever direction was needed. Frey was also linked to ship burials—historians believe that priests of Frey may have presided over these rituals.

Njörd and Frey were invoked in the words of an oath confirming solemn land contracts. The words were spoken over a holy, bloodstained ring that appears in other contracts from Scandinavia to Iceland. Njörd's name was connected from ancient times to the land, which would be tainted by false swearing. The sacred ring was probably an arm ring, since one hero was saved from a sword stroke by wearing it. Later, it appears in literature as a smaller finger ring, but it retains its significance as a symbol of wholeness, prosperous land, and fidelity.

Freya

Njörd's daughter, Freya, was another important deity. As goddess of love and beauty, Freya lived with the Aesir but she also belonged to the Vanir. Freya featured in several important stories. In one, the giant Thrym stole Mjöllnir, the magic hammer of the thunder god Thor. Thrym hid the hammer and refused to return it unless the gods gave him Freya as a bride. The gods tricked Thrym by sending Thor dressed in woman's clothing instead. Thor subsequently killed the giant and regained his hammer. Another giant who sought the hand of Freya was the anonymous master builder. The Aesir promised him that he could marry Freya if he could build them a fortified citadel before the end of winter. It was only through the trickery of the god Loki that Freya escaped this fate.

Stories such as these show the importance of Freya to the Aesir and her central role in Norse mythology. As a goddess of love, she was the most widely worshiped Norse goddess, even more so than Frigga, the wife of Odin. Confusingly, Freya's identity sometimes merges with that of Frigga. Freya also has links to the Germanic fertility goddess Nethus, who is sometimes seen as the sister and consort of Njörd.

BARBARA GARDNER

Bibliography

Larrington, Carolyne, trans. *The Poetic Edda*. New York: Oxford University Press, 1996.

Lindow, John. *Norse Mythology: A Guide to the Gods, Heroes, Rituals, and Beliefs*. New York: Oxford University Press, 2002.

Snorri Sturluson, and Anthony Faulkes, trans. *Edda*. New York: Oxford University Press, 1991.

SEE ALSO: Aesir; Balder; Death and the Afterlife; Frey; Freya; Frigga; Loki; Osiris; Scandinavia; Sea; Thor; Vanir.

NORNS

In Norse mythology the Norns, whose collective name means "fates," were three mysterious female figures. Like the Greek Fates, the Norns wove, measured, and cut the rope of destiny, thus determining the fate of humans and other beings.

Below: The three Norns clutch at the rope of destiny in this illustration by Arthur Rackham (1867–1939). The rope breaks, indicating that the fall of the gods, Ragnarok, is imminent. Urd, Verdandi, and Skuld have been depicted as transparent because their control of destiny is nearly over and soon they will no longer exist.

The three principal Norns were Urd, Verdandi, and Skuld. According to Icelandic poet Snorri Sturluson (1179–1241), they lived in Asgard, the home of the Aesir, at the base of Yggdrasil, the World Tree. The Norns' individual names are connected with the past, present, and future. *Urd* means "becoming," *Verdandi* signifies "being," while *Skuld* has been interpreted as "that-which-is-to-be." *Skuld* is also related to the idea of a debt to be paid. For the Norse, death was seen as the price everyone had to pay for the privilege of living.

Role in mythology

In myth, the Norns came to Asgard from Jotunheim, the home of the Giants. Once they had settled beneath Yggdrasil, they attended to their task of weaving the rope that measured both individual lives and the destiny of the universe. The Norns were also responsible for the protection of Yggdrasil itself. They did this by creating a sacred paste from springwater and magic clay and gravel, which they spread over the tree's roots to prevent them from rotting.

The Aesir—the chief Norse deities—were wary of the Norns. Before the Norns arrived, the gods had existed in a timeless state; the arrival of Urd, Verdandi, and Skuld, however, introduced the concept of time and fate to Asgard itself. The gods feared—as did the Scandinavians who worshiped them—a sequence of events that would end in the apocalyptic battle of Ragnarok, the doom of the gods, and the end of the world. Despite their apprehension, the Aesir journeyed daily to the home of the Norns. At the Well of Urd, beneath Yggdrasil, the gods met to debate how they could delay the inevitable coming of Ragnarok.

Urd, Verdandi, and Skuld were not the only Norns. According to Snorri, there were also countless others, belonging to different races. Snorri suggested that there were three different races. The first race was descended from the Aesir and controlled the lives of humans. The second race was descended from, and controlled the lives of, elves; while the third race was descended from dwarfs and regulated their destinies. Adding a further level of complexity to the description, Snorri also stated that all Norns could be divided into two types: good and bad. If one's life was shaped by a good Norn, it would be happy and fulfilling; if a bad Norn was responsible, life would be miserable.

Death and destiny

In keeping with traditional Norse warrior culture, the Norns were particularly concerned with the destinies of those who fought and died in battle. However, their responsibilities did not include removing the souls of dead heroes from the battlefield. This task was handled by the Valkyries, birdlike female figures that flew over battles. The harsh nature of life in early Scandinavia and the belief in Valhalla, the hall where dead warriors could feast and make merry, may have helped to make the prospect of death less horrific for the Norse than it was for other peoples. As a result, deities such as the Norns, who offered those who believed in them the hope of eternal feasting and fighting, could not ultimately be dreaded since they represented a means of escaping the pain and suffering of earthly life.

Predicting the Future

Like seers in many ancient myths, the Norns could see into the future and predict events for those who consulted them. Some accounts portrayed the Norns as wise old women who traveled around the countryside telling the fortunes of farmers. Other figures in Norse mythology were also able to predict the future. The earth goddess Erda, for example, foresaw the fall of the gods at Ragnarok and conveyed this prediction to the chief of the gods, Odin. An overriding theme in many of the predictions about the future was randomness. The Norse believed that the gods played board games with gold pieces, which symbolized the arbitrary judgments that spelled out the destiny of individuals.

Below: Ship prows and a runic inscription carved in wood commemorate a Viking journey. Some Vikings believed that the Norns carved people's destinies into wood.

In many ancient cultures, people assumed that their destiny was predetermined by gods or by their own actions in previous lives. The idea of free will developed relatively late. Even in the Middle Ages, Christian beliefs combined the concept of free will with an element of predetermination—the idea that a person's fate was decided before or at birth. Perhaps the brutal living conditions and short lifespan of people in the ancient and medieval periods inclined them to think that control over one's destiny was a foolish notion.

Psychologically, belief in fate may have been comforting to those who could not change the painful, limiting conditions of their daily life. Myths and fairy tales abound with heroes and heroines who receive arbitrary help or punishment from external sources over which they have no control. This view of life as a given, beyond the power of humans to shape it by their own initiative, seems to have been held in many ancient societies. It explains, for instance, the parallels between the Norns and the Greek Fates: Clotho, who spun the thread of life; Lachesis, who measured it; and Atropos, who cut the thread.

Barbara Gardner

Bibliography

Lindow, John. *Norse Mythology: A Guide to the Gods, Heroes, Rituals, and Beliefs.* New York: Oxford University Press, 2002.

Snorri Sturluson, and Anthony Faulkes, trans. *Edda.* New York: Oxford University Press, 1991.

See also: Aesir; Apocalypse Myths; Death and the Afterlife; Fates; Odin; Scandinavia; Valkyries.

NUT

In ancient Egypt the goddess Nut was known as mother sky. Her body was both the day and the night sky, and the sun god traveled across and through her eternally. Each night at sunset Nut ate the sun, only to give birth to him the next morning. The lifeblood shed by the sun when the goddess consumed him in the evening gave the sky its red color at sunset, while the birth blood that flowed from Nut when she bore the sun again next morning gave the sunrise a similar hue.

The ancient Egyptians had many creation myths, and in almost all of them the sky goddess Nut was one of the primordial deities. Many ancient cultures conceived of the sky as something solid, a firmament that arched over the (flat) earth. For the ancient Egyptians, Nut's body was this firmament. She was the starry sky and the eternal mother of the sun, and she played an important role in keeping the cosmos organized. Her connection with the stars linked her to the organization of the day and night into hours, the calculation of the year, and the progression of the seasons.

Keeping chaos at bay
In the Egyptian creation stories the universe began as a watery chaos known as Nun. From this arose a creator, identified in ancient Egyptian theology with a number of gods. This deity established the world as the Egyptians knew it, creating the sky and the earth and other elements, as well as humans and animals. Afterward, although the creator deity had organized things to some extent, chaos still existed. One of Nut's major functions was to keep the world of gods and mortals from contact with each other, otherwise it was thought that anarchy would reign.

According to the oldest preserved creation myth, which appears in the Pyramid Texts (about 2400 BCE), the creator god was Atum. The Pyramid Texts were collections of spells that were written on the walls of entrances to tombs—later these spells were written on papyrus and known as Books of the Dead. In the beginning the creator was alone in a watery chaos. Atum then brought forth from himself two other deities: Shu, god of air and sunshine, and Tefnut, goddess of moisture. These two elemental gods produced Nut, goddess of the sky, and her husband and brother, Geb, the earth god. Nut and Geb in turn had four children: Isis, Osiris, Seth, and Nepthys. Those four deities were the core of the ancient Egyptian mythic system, which was used as a model for the kingship, the cycles of nature, and the death and rebirth of human beings.

The mother of all gods
Egyptian mythology, like Greek and Roman mythology, often offered many versions of the same events. Thus although Nut was always seen as the mate of Geb and mother of Isis, Osiris, Seth, and Nepthys, she was also described as both "mother of all the gods" and "mother of the sun god."

Different versions of events developed because myths evolved over 3,000 years, and because priests of various deities desired to make their own local god or goddess more prominent and important. This desire also led priests to identify one god with another and merge their personalities. For example, since Re was probably the most prominent and ancient god of the pantheon, Horus merged with him to become Re-horakhty, while Amun absorbed many of Re's characteristics to become Amun-Re.

Nut appears in three main forms: as the personification of the sky, as one of the judges of the dead, and as the heavenly cow. The most common of these forms is a naked woman whose star-studded body was depicted stretched across the ceilings of temples and royal tombs, and even inside sarcophagi (stone coffins). In the royal tombs of the 19th and 20th Egyptian dynasties (about 1200 to 1000 BCE), Nut's image is doubled to show that she is both the day and the night sky.

Left: This illustration from the lid of a sarcophagus shows the goddess Nut arching her body over the world. It dates from the fourth century BCE. Here the world is shown as a sphere; in earlier art it was usually depicted as the body of Nut's husband, Geb.

Except for the stars that are scattered across her body, in this form the goddess had no crowns or other insignia. The stars and her position, outstretched across the lid or ceiling, were sufficient to identify her—there was never any other deity who filled this role.

Illustrations from Books of the Dead also depict Nut's husband, Geb. He is shown lying prone, or raised on one elbow, beneath his wife. The couple are separated by their father, Shu, who stands between them holding up the body of the goddess. Sometimes their mother, Tefnut, is also shown standing upon the body of Geb.

In this form Nut was not only the vehicle for the sun's daily rebirth, and for the rebirth of Osiris and his representative the king, but also eventually for all Egyptians. In Books of the Dead her belly is described as a "secret cavern" through which the sun passes at night. Few intact royal burials have been found, but probably most New Kingdom (c. 1540–c. 1075 BCE) pharaohs were buried inside two or more mummy-shaped coffins of rich materials, contained within a rectangular sarcophagus. On the inside lid of a number of these royal sarcophagi, Nut was depicted outstretched above the king.

In some of these images Nut was shown holding her breast. The milk of various goddesses was necessary to assist the king at crucial stages in his life: for example, at birth, at his coronation, and on his journey into the afterlife. According to ancient Egyptian hymns and prayers, Nut offered this milk to the king so that he would be restored to youth when he had (symbolically) passed through her body to be reborn. Royal tombs in ancient Egypt were intended to mirror the sun's journey to rebirth. Because he was believed to be son of the sun god, the pharaoh was also entitled to immortality via the goddess's body. Thus, the tomb, sarcophagus, and coffins themselves might also be seen as representations of Nut.

Other forms of Nut

While the image of Nut as the personification of sky was the most easily recognizable and popular one, she also appeared in other forms. In copies of the Book of the Dead made for wealthy, nonroyal individuals, Nut might also have appeared as one of the judges of the dead. After death, human beings were called to the underworld to have their hearts weighed against a feather symbolizing cosmic order (Maat). Osiris presided over this ceremony, and Thoth, god of wisdom, history, and writing, kept a record of the results. Twelve other gods and goddesses formed a jury. Among them were Geb, Tefnut, Shu, and Nut.

Below: This wall painting from a 13th-century-BCE tomb shows an Egyptian couple kneeling before the goddess Nut, who is emerging from a sycamore tree. Nut was closely associated with the sycamore.

Nut was also visualized as the heavenly cow. As with the most common of her human forms, this image of Nut depicted her body covered with stars. As the heavenly cow, Nut could do many of the things her human form could also do. For example, she could give milk, which helped restore the deceased king or sun god, and give birth.

Egyptian cattle, including cows, were all horned, and the horns of the heavenly cow caught the sun at sunset and held him as he began his nighttime journey. The idea that the sky deity was a horned cow probably derived from the similarity in shape of the curved horns of the heavenly cow and the valleys in the cliffs along the Nile. All along the river the habitable land is bracketed by cliffs. These cliffs are broken up by wadis, the valleys left by rivers that flowed many thousands of years ago. Often, as the sun in Egypt rises or sets, it appears on the horizon framed by the rock walls of a wadi.

Other cow deities

In her cow form Nut could be compared to other deities who could take bovine shape, and eventually she was identified with more than one of them. For example, one

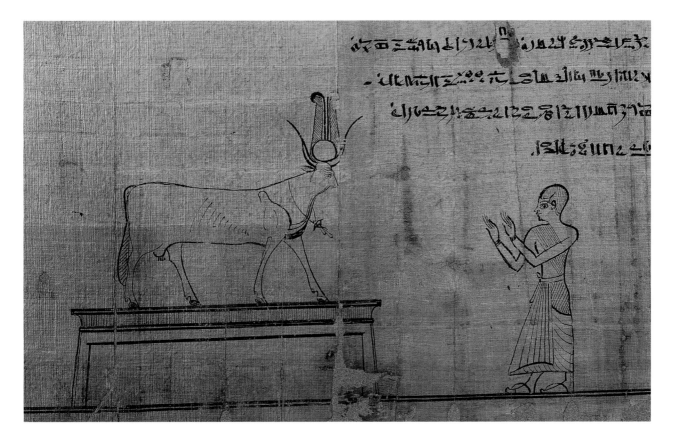

Above: This illustration from a Book of the Dead dating from the first century BCE shows the goddess Nut in her cow form.

version of the Book of the Dead makes reference to a seemingly unnamed cow goddess who emerged from the primordial waters to initiate the creation of the organized universe of gods and humans. She is sometimes known to scholars as the "great swimmer."

Another cow goddess was Hesat. Some myths say that she gave birth to the king in the form of a calf. She has been described as a milk goddess, although her udders apparently produced a heavenly liquid more like beer. She was worshiped because this liquid could quench the thirst of all humankind.

The most important of the other cow deities, however, was Hathor. As a sky goddess and a mother goddess, she was always one of the most important of the Egyptian pantheon, and she was one of the goddesses who eventually absorbed Nut's personality and duties. Although she often appeared as a beautiful woman, she could be shown with cow ears or even entirely in the form of a cow.

Hathor was also lady of the southern sycamore, a tree that had great symbolic value in ancient Egypt. Its wood was often used to make coffins, and thus many funerary goddesses, including Isis and Nut, were also identified as ladies of the sycamore. As lady of the sycamore a goddess would be depicted as a sycamore tree with arms emerging from it, or as a woman emerging from the top of the tree.

Nut is mentioned in the Pyramid Texts, the slightly later Coffin Texts, and the Books of the Dead, and she is widely represented on tomb ceilings, coffins, and sarcophagi. However, for a goddess of such antiquity and importance there are surprisingly few references to her in Egyptian myths. Unlike most other Egyptian gods and goddesses of creation, Nut had no special city or cult center. The reason for this may have been because, in many cultures, deities associated with the underworld, and thus with the earth, did not have formal temples. However, in some temples built by the Greek and Roman rulers of Egypt, there are chapels to Nut. Unfortunately, these chapels cannot tell us much about the way Nut was originally worshiped, since by the time the Romans ruled Egypt, Nut had been absorbed by other goddesses, such as Hathor.

LYN GREEN

Bibliography

Redford, Donald B. *The Oxford Essential Guide to Egyptian Mythology.* New York: Oxford University Press, 2003.
Wilkinson, Richard H. *The Complete Gods and Goddesses of Ancient Egypt.* New York: Thames and Hudson, 2003.

SEE ALSO: Atum; Book of the Dead; Creation Myths; Egypt; Geb; Horus; Isis; Nepthys; Osiris; Re; Seth.

NYMPHS

In Greek and Roman mythology, nymphs were female spirits of great beauty. There were many different types of nymphs: among the most famous were the Dryads, Naiads, and Nereids.

Each type of nymph inhabited a particular natural feature: Dryads lived in forests, especially in oak trees; Naiads dwelled in freshwater lakes, rivers, and springs; Nereids lived in the Mediterranean Sea. Other types of nymphs settled in grottoes, mountains, oceans, and valleys. Nymphs passed their time in harmless leisure pursuits, such as bathing, dancing, singing, and weaving. Most nymphs lived in harmony with all other beings except satyrs, whose lustful advances nymphs often had to repel.

The beauty of nymphs never faded, so they gave the impression that they were immortal. This was misleading, however, since many nymphs died at the same time as their habitats: a Hamadryad would perish when the tree in which she lived died, and a Naiad would disappear when her spring ran dry. The ancient Greeks and Romans worshiped nymphs at nymphaeums (huge fountains built near wells).

Many nymphs had love affairs with gods or men, and many of these liaisons produced children. For example, the nymph Harmonia and the war god Ares were the parents of the Amazons, a race of warrior women. The Charites or Graces, personifications of charm and beauty, were the children of the Naiad Aegle and the sun god Helios. Another Naiad, Lara, and the god Hermes were the parents of the Lares, twin brothers who guarded crossroads and kept watch over cities. The water nymph

Below: This fresco from Stabiae, an ancient town in Italy, depicts a reclining Nereid. Nymphs were often portrayed naked or partially clothed to convey their attractiveness to gods and men.

12 Types of Nymphs

Name	Description or habitat
Atlantid:	Any of the offspring of Atlas
Dryad:	Forests and trees, particularly oaks
Hamadryad:	Trees
Hyad:	Any daughter of Atlas and Aethra; a sister of Hyas
Limniad:	Lakes, marshes, and swamps; dangerous to travelers
Limoniad:	Meadows and flowers
Naiad:	Freshwater lakes, rivers, and springs
Napaea:	Valleys with grazing herds
Nereid:	The Mediterranean Sea in general and the Aegean Sea in particular
Oceanid:	Oceans; also fountains and streams
Oread:	Mountains and grottoes
Pleiad:	Any one of the seven daughters of Atlas and Pleione

Right: This illustration of Calypso and Odysseus by H. J. Ford (1860–1941) depicts the nymph taking pity on the homesick hero. After seven years of captivity on her island, Calypso was instructed by Hermes to release Odysseus so that he might return home to his wife, Penelope.

Melite had a liaison with Heracles and gave birth to Hyllus. Several nymphs married kings and cofounded important dynasties.

The myth of Pomona

One particularly famous nymph was Pomona, a Dryad who confined herself to an apple orchard and was not interested in gods or men. Despite her precautions, Vertumnus, the Roman god of change and the seasons, managed to seduce her. When Vertumnus first appeared to her as a reaper, haymaker, and vine pruner, he was unable to win her heart. So he disguised himself as an old woman, complimented Pomona on her beauty, and kissed her. The old woman then listed the reasons why Vertumnus would make an ideal husband, but Pomona remained unmoved. Finally, Vertumnus assumed his true form and Pomona fell in love with him. The myth of Pomona and Vertumnus has inspired many artists, including Flemish sculptor Laurent Delvaux (1695–1778). Delvaux's statue of the couple shows Vertumnus revealing his true form to Pomona but holding a mask with an old woman's face on it.

The Naiads and Nereids

Some Naiads were the daughters of Zeus, while others were the daughters of various river gods or members of the vast family of the Titan Oceanus. According to classical mythology, waters frequented by Naiads had inspirational, medicinal, or prophetic powers. Naiads who lived in the rivers of Hades were known as the Avernales or *Nymphae Infernae Paludis*, "Nymphs of the Infernal Swamp." One of these was the Naiad Lara, daughter of the river god Almo. When Lara reported to Hera that Zeus loved Juturna, Zeus tore out her tongue as a punishment. He then had Hermes take her to Hades, where she became an infernal nymph known as Tacita, "the Silent One."

There are many other Naiad myths. Hylas was a handsome young mortal, an Argonaut, and a companion of Heracles. Returning from one of their many adventures, the Argonauts stopped at an island and Hylas went ashore to fetch fresh water. By a spring in Bithynia (in modern Turkey), Hylas discovered nymphs. The Naiads who lived in the spring fell in love with Hylas and lured him into the

Right: This fifth-century-BCE silver coin from Syracuse in Sicily bears the head of the nymph Arethusa, one of the Hesperides.

waters for eternity. According to different versions of the myth, Hylas was either drowned or experienced everlasting sexual bliss.

One notable group of four Naiads was known as the Hesperides. Their names were Aegle, Arethusa, Erytheia, and Hesperia. These four sisters guarded the golden apple tree that Gaia gave to Hera as a wedding present. It was from this tree that Heracles stole the golden apples as his 11th labor.

Another myth recounts how the Naiad Salmacis loved handsome Hermaphroditus, a son of Aphrodite and Hermes. When Hermaphroditus swam in the spring of Salmacis (close to Halicarnassus in Asia Minor), Salmacis embraced him and prayed that they never be separated. The gods took pity and fused the two of them into a single body. Hermaphroditus asked the gods to make any man who bathed in the spring lose his virility, and the gods agreed. This myth provided an explanation for dual sexuality and produced another myth: anyone who bathed in or drank from the Salmacis spring would be rendered effeminate.

The Nereids were the 50 daughters of Nereus, the god of the Mediterranean Sea, and his sea goddess wife, Doris.

Nereids were beautiful, friendly, and helpful to sailors during perilous storms. One notable Nereid was Thetis, the mother of Achilles. The goddess Themis prophesied that Thetis would have a son mightier than his father. Zeus had lusted after Thetis, but, fearing the prophecy, he made her marry the mortal Peleus. Thetis gave birth to Achilles, whom she tried to make immortal. In a popular version of the myth, Thetis held her baby by one heel and dipped him in the Styx, the chief river of the underworld. Achilles' body became almost invulnerable—his only weak point was his heel. In another account, Thetis anointed Achilles with ambrosia and tried to hold him over a fire to burn away his mortality. Achilles' father Peleus was horrified and intervened to stop her. In another myth, Thetis protected Achilles by giving him invincible armor made by Hephaestus, the smith god. Despite wearing the armor, the hero was killed during the Trojan War when Apollo guided an arrow shot by Paris directly into Achilles' heel. On a sixth-century-BCE Corinthian vase, Nereids dressed in mourning weep over Achilles on his deathbed.

Other nymphs

The sea deities Oceanus and Tethys had more than 3,000 daughters known as Oceanids. The Oceanid Perse was said to be mother to a number of famous figures in Greek mythology, including Calypso, Aeetes, Circe, and Pasiphae. Calypso and Circe encountered Odysseus after the Trojan War; Pasiphae was the mother of the fearsome Minotaur; and Aeetes was a fierce king who set a dragon to guard the Golden Fleece. The Greek island of Rhodes was named for the oldest Oceanid, Rhode. Astronomers named one of Jupiter's moons for the Oceanid Telesto, and the continent of Asia was named for another, Asia. An Oceanid named Pleione was the mother of the seven Pleiades, who were sisters immortalized in the night sky as a cluster of seven stars.

Many nymphs met tragic fates as a result of the amorous attentions of Zeus, king of the gods. One was Callisto, a huntress and sworn virgin who was faithfully devoted to the goddess Artemis. One day Callisto was raped by Zeus. Hera, angered by her husband's infidelity, avenged herself on Callisto. When Callisto gave birth to her son Arcas, Hera transformed the nymph into a bear. Arcas grew up to be a hunter, and years later encountered his mother. Callisto, forgetting her changed shape, recognized her son and tried to hug him. Arcas was frightened and took aim at her, but Zeus felt sorry for Callisto and placed her in the sky as the constellation Ursa Major (great bear). He then turned Arcas into a star and placed him near his mother. Zeus's action infuriated Hera, who asked her nurse Tethys to curse Callisto and Arcas by depriving them of water. As a result, they never dipped below the horizon into the ocean for a refreshing bath or a cool drink. For the ancient Greeks this myth accounted for the fact that Ursa Major and Ursa Minor were visible all year round.

In another myth, Echo the mountain nymph was a servant to Hera. Zeus persuaded Echo to distract his wife with endless chatter while he courted other women. Hera discovered Echo's ploy and deprived the nymph of original speech, condemning her to repeat only the last words she heard. Later, Echo fell in love with beautiful Narcissus, but, unable to declare her love, pined away until nothing was left except her voice.

The gods often transformed nymphs into natural objects. Syrinx was a river nymph pursued by Pan; she fled into her river where the gods changed her into a reed. Pan cut the reed into various pieces and made the musical pipes on which he played. The nymph Chelone ridiculed the

Cyrene

The nymph Cyrene was the daughter of the Naiad Creusa and the mortal Hypseus, king of Lapith and the son of the river god Peneius. Cyrene hated womanly arts; she hunted, practiced javelin and swordplay, and protected her father's herds. Apollo fell in love with her when he saw her wrestle a lion that attacked her father's sheep. Apollo consulted Cheiron, the civilized centaur known for his wisdom, on the best way to woo Cyrene. Cheiron predicted that Apollo would make his beloved the ruler of a great city, and that they would have a son who would become immortal. Apollo took Cyrene to Libya, where he built a city that bore her name. Their son Aristaeus became a pastoral deity, patron of hunting, cattle, olive cultivation, and beekeeping.

Other sources said Cyrene was a mortal whom Apollo kidnapped while she tended sheep along the Peneius River. He took her to live with nymphs near the Myrtosian height in Libya. When Aristaeus was born, Apollo sent him to be raised by Cheiron, and made Cyrene a nymph because nymphs live longer than mortals. According to another myth, Cyrene and the war god Ares were the parents of King Diomedes of Thrace, who owned the man-eating mares that Heracles stole as one of his 12 labors.

Below: Pillars of a sanctuary of Apollo still stand among ruins of the city of Cyrene. According to legend, the city was named after the nymph of the same name.

Clytie and Apollo

Clytie was a beautiful water nymph who loved Apollo. When Apollo seduced the mortal woman Leucothoe, jealous Clytie told Leucothoe's father, who then buried Leucothoe alive. Apollo, angered and saddened by Leucothoe's death, still refused to love Clytie. For nine days, Clytie sat on the cold ground and pined for him. She did not eat or drink; her tears and the chilly dew were her only nourishment. With her long hair streaming about her face, she gazed on Apollo when he rose and watched him all day until he set on the far horizon. At last, Clytie's limbs became roots and her face became a sunflower, always turning to face the sun. The myth was the inspiration for a poem about the constancy of love written by Irish poet Thomas Moore (1779–1852).

Below: The myth of Apollo and Clytie offers an explanation for why sunflowers turn their heads to follow the sun.

wedding of Zeus and Hera, so the gods condemned her to eternal silence by turning her into a turtle. Arethusa, one of the Hesperides, fled to Sicily when the river god Alpheus fell in love with her. Artemis changed Arethusa into a fountain (the Fonte Aretusa in Syracuse), but Alpheus went beneath the sea and merged his waters with hers. The head of Arethusa, encircled by dolphins, was depicted on coins from Syracuse in about the fifth century BCE.

Mortal women could sometimes become nymphs. Apollo's granddaughter Byblis fell in love with her own brother (in some myths, Byblis's brother conceived a passion for her). Different versions of the myth have different outcomes. One says that Byblis was transformed into a fountain of her own tears, another that she turned into a Hamadryad. According to a third account, Byblis killed herself, while yet another states that she became a spring created from tears shed for her son Cenchrias, whom Artemis had accidentally killed.

One myth recounts how the mountain nymph Daphne was struck by one of Eros's arrows. The god of sexual love, Eros was angered by Apollo's taunts and fired two arrows: one was gold-tipped and struck Apollo, filling him with insatiable lust. The other struck Daphne, but it was lead-tipped and caused abhorrence. Desperately in love, Apollo chased Daphne, but she ran from him until she grew weary. She called to her father, the river god Peneius, for help, and he transformed her into a laurel tree. Still enamored, Apollo claimed the laurel as his tree; and from this point on he was adorned with laurel leaves.

ALYS CAVINESS

Bibliography

Apollodorus, and Robin Hard, trans. *The Library of Greek Mythology.* New York: Oxford University Press, 1999.

SEE ALSO: Achilles; Apollo; Callisto; Calypso; Daphne; Dryads; Hera; Heracles; Narcissus; Pan; Peleus; Thetis; Zeus.

NYX

Nyx (also spelled Nux) was the ancient Greek goddess of night. Born from Chaos, the primordial darkness, Nyx herself gave birth to a host of deities. She also shared with her daughter Hemera (Day) a home in the underworld, but the two goddesses were never there at the same time. Each day, while Hemera passed over the earth, Nyx rested until it was her time to bring darkness to the world.

Nyx had many children, most of whom personified negative aspects of the human condition. They included the Keres (Doom), Thanatos (Death), Hypnos (Sleep), Oneiroi (Dreams), Nemesis (Retribution), Geras (Old Age), Eris (Discord), Apate (Deceit), and Philotes (Desire). She also gave birth to the three Fates—Clotho, Lachesis, and Atropos—who measured out each person's lifespan; and to the Hesperides—Aegle, Erytheia, Hesperia, and Arethusa—whose golden apples were stolen by Heracles. Nyx's other children—Aether (Brightness) and Hemera (Day)—were by her brother, Erebus (Darkness).

Below: Nyx appears in this scene from a Greek bas-relief of the second century BCE depicting the battle between Olympians and Titans.

Above: This painting by Edward Burne-Jones (1833–1898) shows the garden of the Hesperides. The Hesperides were daughters of Nyx who guarded a tree that bore golden apples. Here they are depicted dancing around it.

Nyx lived in Tartarus, the deepest part of the underworld, where she shared with Hemera a house with a threshold of bronze. Other inhabitants of Tartarus included Nyx's children Hypnos and Thanatos.

Most ancient Greeks probably became acquainted with the details of this version of Nyx's story through hearing performances of an ancient Greek epic called *Theogony*; the title means "birth of the gods" in Greek. The poem, attributed to Greek poet Hesiod (fl. 800 BCE), is one of the earliest surviving examples of Greek literature. *Theogony* offered a view of the gods that brought together many local traditions about the origins and nature of the gods. Most Greeks recognized Hesiod's version of Greek mythology as being authoritative.

Orphic versions of Nyx's story

There were other versions of Nyx's origins besides Hesiod's, however. For example, adherents to Orphism, an obscure religious sect, made Nyx the daughter of a creator god named Phanes. According to this version, Nyx and Phanes had an incestuous relationship that produced Uranus, who in the mainstream account of Greek mythology was the son of Gaia (Earth). Nyx served first as Uranus's adviser, then as adviser to Uranus's son, Cronus, and finally to Cronus's son, Zeus, when he became ruler of the Olympian gods.

In another version of the Orphic story, Nyx laid an egg, from which hatched Phanes and other deities. Some scholars suggest that Nyx may have been the supreme deity in an earlier phase of Orphic belief, and there is evidence that some Greeks considered her the original creator deity.

Most Greek deities that personified the natural world and aspects of existence remained relatively minor figures in Greek mythology, and this is largely true of Nyx. Although she features in the Orphic liturgy, there is little evidence that Nyx was worshiped with temples and sacrifices, as were major Olympian deities such as Zeus and Athena. On the other hand, Greek travel writer Pausanias (143–176 CE) mentions an oracle of Nyx in Megara, a Greek city west of Athens.

Witches in Greek myths sometimes prayed to Nyx, suggesting that ancient magicians may have invoked her in curses and spells. As for the arts, no play or hymn is known to have been devoted to Nyx, and there are few depictions of her in Greek painting or sculpture.

As a symbol of darkness and night, Nyx was believed to have enormous power. In the epic poem the *Iliad* by Greek poet Homer (c. ninth–eighth century BCE), a story told by Nyx's son Hypnos is evidence of this power. Hera, Zeus's

wife and queen of the Olympian gods, hated the hero Heracles because he was Zeus's son by a mortal woman. One day she decided to wreck Heracles' ships. In order to distract Zeus from her deed, Hera persuaded Hypnos to make Zeus fall asleep. Hera then sent a storm against Heracles' fleet. When Zeus awoke, he flew into a rage because he knew he had been sent to sleep by Hypnos, and he began searching for him. Zeus was intent on hurling the god of sleep from Mount Olympus, but Hypnos fled to his mother, Nyx, for protection. When Zeus learned that Hypnos was with Nyx, he abandoned his pursuit because he was unwilling to do anything that would displease Nyx.

Personification in myths

Ancient Greek myths contain numerous references to deities who are also personifications of things or concepts. Thus, *nyx* as a common noun is the ancient Greek word for "night," and *hypnos* is the Greek word for "sleep."

Many of these personifications belong, like Nyx and her offspring, to a family that is older in the chronological timeline of Greek mythology than the Olympian family ruled by Zeus. The most fundamental elements of the universe appear earliest in this timeline. So it is that the first generation of gods brings forth Chaos, the dark void; Gaia, the earth from which all else springs forth to fill the void; and Eros, the impulse to procreate. Nyx is among the second generation of gods, the offspring of Chaos, who represents the all-engulfing darkness of the heavens. Nyx personifies the specific darkness experienced on earth at night.

In mythology these pre-Olympian gods tend to be grouped into subfamilies of related ideas and concepts. Ideas that are connected by the circumstances in which they tend to occur—such as night, sleep, and dreams—are represented as close kin. Thus Nyx's offspring include the personification of sleep (Hypnos) and dreams (Oneiroi).

Family relationships can also represent more general connections among abstract ideas. Since night is a time when people tend to feel more vulnerable, or helpless, the goddess Nyx is viewed as the matriarch of a family of concepts that impose limits on human power, such as death, old age, and fate. Nyx was also the mother of concepts such as strife, deception, and sexual desire—ideas that often come to mind during dreams and that reflect a darker side of human nature.

A similar way of thinking can be seen in the way people used the names of major gods to refer to broad concepts. Ancient Greek poets, for example, used the name of the

Left: Darkness falls on the island of Santorini. Ancient Greeks believed that Nyx was the goddess of night.

war god Ares to mean "war." Likewise, a common way to say "it's raining" in ancient Greece was *Zeus huei*, meaning "Zeus is making water."

Coming to terms with abstract concepts

In cosmological myths (those relating to the nature of the universe) and cosmogonic myths (those relating to the origins and development of the universe), personification was a useful way for the ancients to think about abstract concepts. In turn, the system of relationships among human families was as a useful way to organize these concepts.

Ancient Greek philosophers also used personification to rationalize ideas in poetry that seemed strange or irreligious to them. The battles among the gods during the Trojan War, for example, were interpreted as an allegory that described the relationships among the constituent elements of the universe as the Greeks saw them. The clash between the fire god Hephaestus and a river god in the *Iliad*, for example, represented the opposing natures of fire and water.

Personification in ancient myths reveals a complex and systematic way of understanding the world. The religious systems and myths of cultures the world over feature sun gods, moon gods, and so on, and relate them to one another as members of the same mythological family.

The personified concept of night has a place in the religions of a number of other cultures, too. The pre-Hindu Vedic texts of ancient India, for example, recognized a night goddess. She, like Nyx, was associated with phenomena of the heavens, being the sister of the dawn and daughter of the sky. The Roman name for the goddess of the night was Nox. Most of the evidence we have for Nox shows the influence of the Greek Nyx.

JIM MARKS

Bibliography

Apollodorus, and Robin Hard, trans. *The Library of Greek Mythology.* New York: Oxford University Press, 1999.

Graves, Robert. *The Greek Myths.* New York: Penguin USA, 1993.

Hesiod, and M. L. West, ed. *Theogony; and Works and Days.* New York: Oxford University Press, 1999.

Howatson, M. C., and Ian Chilvers. *Concise Oxford Companion to Classical Literature.* New York: Oxford University Press, 1993.

Ovid, and A. D. Melville, trans. *Metamorphoses.* New York: Oxford University Press, 1998.

SEE ALSO: Cronus; Fates; Gaia; Hera; Heracles; Hesperides; Hypnos; Nemesis; Uranus; Zeus.

INDEX

Page numbers in *italics* refer to picture captions. Page numbers in **bold** refer to main articles.